"*Supporting College and University Students with Invisible Disabilities* provides clear and focused explanations of important concepts in the field of disability. This is information that all administrators and faculty should know when working with students with invisible disabilities. The chapters provide necessary legal explanations, address the myths around invisible disability, and provide useful guides and strategies to help administrators and faculty work with students. As an administrator and faculty member, I found this text invaluable. I highly recommend it."

—K. Alex Ilyasova, Director of the Professional and Technical Writing program in the English Department at the University of Colorado at Colorado Springs

"This book is an invaluable guide for understanding and including students with disabilities in post-secondary institutions. The descriptive information about developmental and emotional issues truly enables the reader to identify with someone struggling with a particular issue, while simultaneously learning scientific and practical applications. The author convincingly identifies the social imperative to improve the way we include students with learning and emotional challenges, and offers provocative ideas for institutional changes that feel doable and make sense."

—Sarita Freedman, Ph.D, Licensed Psychologist and author of Developing College Skills in Students with Autism and Asperger's Syndrome

"In this book, Dr. Christy Oslund uses academic research, pedagogical experience, and common sense to help faculty, administrators, and staff in academic settings navigate one of the most prevalent issues in higher education today: understanding and accommodating invisible disabilities. Employing a gentle humor immediately relatable to other educators, Oslund provides practical information on how these invisible disabilities affect students, parents, and colleagues while providing actionable ideas for making campuses better environments for everyone."

—Casey J Rudkin, Ph.D, Department of Writing, Linguistics and Creative Process, Western Connecticut State University

D1636674

"This book should be required reading for all higher education instructors. In thoughtful yet practical terms, Dr. Oslund illustrates how to recognize and respond to diverse learners, which is an ethical and moral necessity too often neglected during new teacher orientations and the competing demands of ongoing professional life."

—*Moe Folk, Ph.D, Assistant Professor of English,*
Kutztown University of Pennsylvania

SUPPORTING COLLEGE AND UNIVERSITY STUDENTS WITH INVISIBLE DISABILITIES

SUPPORTING COLLEGE AND UNIVERSITY STUDENTS with INVISIBLE DISABILITIES

A GUIDE FOR FACULTY AND STAFF WORKING WITH STUDENTS WITH AUTISM, AD/HD, LANGUAGE PROCESSING DISORDERS, ANXIETY, AND MENTAL ILLNESS

CHRISTY OSLUND

Jessica Kingsley *Publishers*
London and Philadelphia

First published in 2014
by Jessica Kingsley Publishers
73 Collier Street
London N1 9BE, UK
and
400 Market Street, Suite 400
Philadelphia, PA 19106, USA

www.jkp.com

Library of Congress Cataloging in Publication Data
A CIP catalog record for this book is available from the Library of Congress

British Library Cataloguing in Publication Data
A CIP catalogue record for this book is available from the British Library

ISBN 978 1 84905 955 8
eISBN 978 0 85700 785 8

Printed and bound in Great Britain by Bell & Bain Ltd, Glasgow

This book is dedicated to the people who have taught me in my life. Some had patience, some were exuberant, and some taught by example what not to do. I've also learned a great deal from those whose classroom is in the world outside academia, and from many who thought of themselves first and foremost as students.

My journey on the path of learning continues...

Contents

Introduction

A true story from the classroom

I had recognized the autistic characteristics in the young man from the beginning of the semester. He was in fact, one of three students in the technical communication class I was teaching who I pegged as probably living with Aspergers—the high functioning end of the autism spectrum disorders; he displayed the typical attention to the details that interested him, as well as extensive knowledge in these areas, while also displaying an inability to process social cues and expectations. I wasn't surprised, then that he was *demanding* a different grade, oblivious to the fact that this was not his best rhetorical choice for "persuading" me to see his point of view.

"I have taken an A's worth of knowledge from this class," he insisted.

I nodded and, pressed to be somewhere else, as well as not wanting to sound snippy since I understood the source of his social awkwardness. I responded, "Put your argument in writing and email it to me so that I can respond to it." I'd decided it wouldn't hurt him to have a little more practice with formal written communication and maybe we could at least get one more teachable moment out of the semester.

His argument for a higher grade contained the internal logic I expected and in my response I acknowledged the points he made were valid. I then listed the points that his argument overlooked: he had missed classes in excess of what my attendance policy allowed and as I'd outlined in the syllabus and verbally, attendance counted because one of the class practices was to prepare for the working world where attendance would matter; I also had made it clear throughout the semester that due to each student's specialized background and experience their unique points of view shaped their classmates' learning experience, and not being in class was withholding knowledge from others. I valued presence and thus made it part of the grade he kept or forfeited. I also pointed out the written policy about consistent late arrival counting as an additional absence from class. I summarized my points by stating that it was because of his excellent work product that I had not further penalized his grade given his attendance and proclivity to late arrival.

I was rather surprised when he responded with an apology. He stated that having read my counter-argument he realized he had not looked at this from both sides and that he was in fact benefiting from some beneficence on my part—and thanked me. I share this story to make several points:

- Students on the autism spectrum never cease to surprise me, despite over 14 years of teaching experience with many members of this group.

- Professors are just as well served as students to calmly and rationally make a logical argument, vs. losing our tempers and reverting to, "How many times do I have to tell you…" or other less thoughtful arguments.

While I'm at it I will tag on one further point:

- Having all one's policies clearly spelled out in the syllabus from the very beginning of the semester will save a person time and effort later when someone inevitably complains about a grade they earned by violating one/more of these policies.

Diversity among the similarly disabled

Both as a teacher and an administrator I have worked with invisibly disabled young people who have and have not been formally diagnosed with the disabilities they live with. Sometimes my colleagues—faculty and staff—can become concerned with "recognizing" the disability a student or coworker is living with. I regularly remind people that focusing on the correct label is pointless. Observing an individual's behavior is useful only in what it tells us about what will assist us in communicating with, working with, teaching that person and what their behavior tells us about what is not working and what is not likely to work.

I have a colleague and friend for example, who lives with attention deficit disorder (ADD). Knowing this tells me little, aside from the statistical probability that he will have more difficulty focusing in long, boring meetings…but that describes virtually everyone I've ever been in a meeting with, so what useful information does the label give me? None by itself.

Having worked closely with this person, however, I have observed that he is a very good people person, he does an excellent job of "big picture" thinking, and he can see how another person's strengths and limitations can best be used in specific contexts. I've also learned that if I want him to remember something, he'd better write it down while I'm saying it, or immediately be entering a reminder in his electronic calendar. I know that if I tell him something when I catch him in the hallway between meetings that he will no more remember it then I will remember Pi to the 20th digit. (On a good day I remember the first digit of Pi i.e., 3.)

You might think, "Well, that describes many people; I have so many things on my mind that I might not remember something that was mentioned to me in passing…" The difference is, if you and my friend were both actively working on improving memory, using the same systems, and had equal access to the same memory improvement program, *you* may have the potential for marked memory improvement. With the same amount of time, effort, and training my friend's memory will show marginal change. The way ADD affects his brain keeps his short-term memory from being particularly effective, even with a great deal of time and effort put into improving what he does have.

At the most basic level this is what most invisible disabilities have in common. Due to differences in the brain, an invisibly disabled person's brain in some way is not able to process information the way a "standard" brain does; the differences may impact their memory, anxiety levels, ability to focus, ability to process social cues, ability to process specific types of input, and the length of time input takes to be processed. Even when two individuals share a diagnostic label, such as attention deficit disorder, their brains do not process information in exactly the same way. Consider this in relation to two intelligent people who are in the same field of study. Do all people in the same field find exactly the same questions compelling? Do all share exactly the same kind of research styles? Do all have exactly the same relationship with students? Even "normal brains" process information differently; combine this with our differences in experiences and values and it isn't hard to see that just as humans share commonalities, we also vary from person to person. Disabled people are the same; even when we share common diagnosis we are uniquely quirky, gifted, and limited.

Individuals with the same disability can also have different learning styles. Some people are visual learners, some experiential, and some learn best from listening to explanations. There are dyslexic people who learn best visually, and dyslexic people who learn best experientially or from listening— the same is true for the range of disabled people. Sharing a disability category/label does not mean two individuals share the same learning style. In the class where I had three young men whom I suspected were each on the autism spectrum—they had different learning styles, different levels of practice with standard social skills, and different responses to the expectations in class. In Chapter Three, which will focus on autism spectrum disorders, I will speak more about these differences and several similarities I observed as well.

Audience and intent

This book is written for two groups I am part of: (i) those who teach at the post-secondary level, and thus teach the invisibly disabled; and (ii) staff, particularly administrative staff, and those in the "front line" of dealing with students, whose jobs place them in regular contact with the invisibly disabled students and thus require them to communicate meaningfully and assist these students. In what follows what I say will at times be more focused on either the classroom or the staff responsibilities; however, the overall information is useful to all who work in college and university environments in roles that require contact with students.

The students who I am speaking of are forming a growing percentage of the "disabled" students who are attending school; they far outnumber those disabled students who have what is referred to as "visible" disabilities. The difference between visibly and invisibly disabled students includes those with visible disabilities that can usually be immediately or quickly identified: they use canes or guide dogs; their mobility is limited; they communicate with sign language; they wear hearing aids, etc. An invisibly disabled student can be in a classroom, meeting, or be one of a department's work study students, and one cannot tell by looking at this person that they have a disability. The students I am particularly addressing are the invisibly disabled students who are high functioning, as they are a fast-growing part of the population who are also most likely to lack some of the social skills necessary to seek out the assistance they require. The traits they share include:

- They are intelligent—may have found minimal studying necessary prior to university.

- They are more likely to have language processing disorders comorbid with other disorders.

- They prefer hands-on learning over listening to lectures or reading/writing forms of learning.

- They like to see solid results from the work they do, i.e. building something, solving a problem and having a specific answer, and creating answers to standing problems.

Of course, the strategies and information contained within this book will not be limited to these intellectually capable students; however, it is important for those of us in post-secondary education to realize that this may be the fastest growing segment of our disabled student population. I will explain this in further detail later and at this point will just add that currently according to the Center for Disease Control (CDC 2012a) autism spectrum disorders are now being identified in 1 in 88 young people, and 1 in 54 boys, while ADD is estimated to affect 4–6 percent of the population (ADDA 2012a). According to the CDC, as of December 2012 in the US amongst children from 3–17 years of age, 5.2 million have been diagnosed with AD/HD (attention deficit/hyperactive disorder); 12 percent of boys and 4 percent of girls in this age range are living with this disorder (CDC 2012b). The incidence of these disorders are both on the increase and increasingly likely to be identified, although diagnosis still has a long way to go. For example, it requires 7.8–10 years for a person seeking treatment for bipolar disorder to be correctly diagnosed, which is the first step in receiving adequate treatment (Ghaemia *et al.* 1999; Hirschfeld and Vornick 2004) . This fact flies in the face of the social view that mental illness is currently over-diagnosed or that doctors are "too quick" to diagnosis someone as bipolar.

In the past several years, my colleagues at the Midwestern university where I currently work have been noticing that the accommodation letters I am writing for students are changing. In the past, students' accommodation letters were largely glanced at by faculty because they always said the same thing, "Extended test time" and "Non-distracting test environment." Then someone actually noticed that I was slipping in new requirements like, "Student cannot begin tests after 5:00 p.m." and "Please negotiate missed work when student needs to be absent for medical reasons."

One professor asked me, "Are these new things just temporary?" I think the question was really a way of saying, "Please tell me this isn't what I'm afraid it is—the beginning of many more changes, because I already have so much to do and I'm beginning to suspect that with increasing accommodations will be increasing work."

Unfortunately, my message is mixed.

No, the new and increasing number of accommodations being seen are not temporary. As I will discuss in Chapter One under myths, not everyone is disabled, but everyone's life is going to be touched by disability; please read further to unpack this statement and do not immediately rush to panic. There are sufficient reasons for concern without panicking over the things we still have some control over.

Yes, there are ways that institutionally and individually we can be better prepared for the increasing number of increasingly disabled students. This book will provide practical advice for implementing steps that will assist faculty and staff in preparing for at least some of the inevitable changes as the student body on campuses are changing. And if the mindset of one's campus is to only react and not prepare, then I will provide some practices that can be adopted by administration and faculty once things do start to go pear-shaped.

This book can be used by individuals as a way to be better personally prepared; however, I think it would be even more practical to use this as an opening to campus-wide conversations regarding how to be more proactive when it comes to working with our disabled students. This book ideally should be part of a tool kit of responses that include:

- Reading and discussion groups that include faculty and staff, followed by separate reading groups with students—one cannot have the same discussions once students are in the room, just as we learn new things once students join the conversation.

- Professional seminar groups where successful practices are shared.

- Mentoring partnerships between incoming disabled students and successful peers.

- Professional development sessions where new technologies and techniques that increase elements of universally designed education (removing as many handicapping barriers as possible) are shared.

- Colloquiums where successful, professional disabled adults already working in different fields share the obstacles and assists they found during their university careers—with upper echelon administrators and senior faculty, as well as students, attending and participating in discussions with these people. Universities need to create practices, not just verbal messages that value the presence of invisibly disabled students and colleagues.

- Greater administrative recognition of *invisible* disability as a valued form of diversity, shown through hiring and promotion practices, guest speakers, and supported continuing education opportunities (to name just a few).

Correct terminology

When one works in a university one becomes cognizant that terms of reference fall in and out of favor. Some people may be uncomfortable that I have used the term disabled, instead of differently abled, or different. Allow me to explain. I am part of two further alliances, in addition to teaching and administrating. I am a member of the Association on Higher Education and Disability (AHEAD), the professional association for those who provide services for disabled students; I am myself disabled. In much the same way that the GLBTQ movement moved to reclaim the term "queer", the community of disabled and disabled service providers are reclaiming the term "disabled." There is nothing wrong with being disabled. Our line of thinking is that problems do not necessarily arise directly from our disabilities, rather, we are handicapped by specific contexts. As service providers and educators, our responsibility is to remove those obstacles which handicap a disabled person in any given context. For this reason, we remove high curbs which keep a person in a wheelchair from gaining access to a sidewalk.

We would also argue that placing numerous steps between a disabled student and accommodations in university is another form of handicapping people. As the presenters in one conference session I was in asked, "How many steps does a disabled student on your campus have to take to obtain an education, that a non-disabled student does not have to take?" Requiring invisibly disabled students to regularly be re-tested to certify they remain disabled, when most are living with lifelong disabilities, was a handicapping "step" that universities formerly would regularly require if a student wanted to receive accommodations. More recently, federal law in the US at least has made it clear that this is a form of discrimination which is now illegal. American universities are no longer permitted to arbitrarily insist that students be re-tested for their disability every three years.

University classrooms have typically given an unfair *advantage* to those who learn best by sitting passively and listening to a professor lecture. If we start to develop classroom and grading practices that allow students to learn and demonstrate their knowledge in other ways—for example, attaching smaller laboratory sessions to every large lecture class, so that a student can also practice learning hands-on and has someone more immediate, such as a lab leader to answer questions—then we are removing some of the handicapping conditions for those whose learning styles and perhaps disabilities keep them from doing well in a large lecture-only class setting. When we make knowledge more accessible we are not "dumbing down the curriculum", we are instead working towards undoing generations of favoritism for those who are able to excel at lecture formatted classes, which tend to unfairly favor those who also do well with short-term memory exercises. We also improve learning conditions for a majority of students. I have on numerous occasions given presentations and asked the university professionals in the room how many of them feel they learn best by only sitting in a lecture hall. Typically less than five percent of the audience self-identify this as their ideal learning environment. One does not have to be disabled to do far better with hands-on learning vs. lecture; my own studies along with many others have found that most people learn best when allowed to put new knowledge into practice alongside someone already fluent in the practice being acquired (Dewey 2012; Brice-Heath 2012).

Grading practices also become more balanced when rather than weighting one or two tests as the only measure of success in a class, grades are instead distributed over a wider number and range of student responses. Including homework, labs, and multiple tests when arriving at a grade both pedagogically and practically gives a more accurate picture of what a range of learners are actually learning. I will discuss the reasoning for this further in Chapter Eight. At this juncture my point is simply that a more universal design for teaching is already partially in place, even within some large lecture classes; we simply need to be more mindful of the pedagogical reasons for doing things like distributing grades over multiple types of assignments. If we begin to see the pedagogical implications of practices, we can also bring new insights into what is worthy of trying and which practices we need to revisit.

My goal is not to reinvent the wheel on other campuses. Some readers may already use and have colleagues who use universal design practices in teaching and some administrations may already be very student-focused. Experience has taught me though, that what is happening in one area of campus is almost never universally known in other areas of campus. Departments have much to learn from each other about creating productive learning and effective administrative procedures and policies. By opening further cross-campus discussions I am suggesting we can do more to anticipate at least some of the challenges and strengths that disabled students will bring in increasing numbers to our campuses. The fact is, whether we are better prepared for them or not, the presence of increasingly disabled students on university campuses is only going to intensify for the foreseeable future. And even if others on the campus where one works cannot be convinced that change is inevitable—or should be prepared for—a reader can still use this book as a personal resource.

CHAPTER ONE
Dispelling Myths

"Is it just my imagination, or are doctors diagnosing everything as a disability now? When I was in school it was expected that boys would be boys—now they're ADD."

The gentleman in the audience who was making this observation was causing an interesting mix of responses among other audience members. Some were looking down at their feet, perhaps mortified that he was somehow being politically incorrect. Others nodded in agreement with the observation. Some looked upset or shook their heads. A few people even looked ready to jump to their feet and argue.

This was an audience at a university and I was speaking to them specifically about invisible disabilities. There were people in the audience who themselves live with an invisible disability and they had experienced some of the discrimination that seems to be part of this context. Others in the audience were frustrated at what they perceived to be a lack of distinction between "real" disabilities and "fakers" trying to game the system by posing as disabled—there is a societal myth that it is fairly easy to fake an invisible disability, because unlike a visible disability no one can "see" what is wrong; this is a myth that this entire book will work on dispelling.

For non-invisibly disabled people there can be concern that those who "aren't *really* disabled" are going to abuse systems and take resources that ought to be reserved for those who "are really disabled." This wider social concern carries over into the educational system, where professors worry for example, that students who have accommodations for extended time on tests are gaining an unfair advantage over students who have to work within time constraints in test situations.

For those of us who are invisibly disabled on the other hand, it is easy to get upset with people who would appear to label anyone with an invisible disability as trying to put something over on them—at a minimum hypochondriacs, at worst liars. I always remind myself and others though, that it wasn't so long ago that people didn't even want to see visibly disabled people and the social instinct used to be to hide the visibly disabled in institutions or keep them sequestered in their family homes. It is instinctual to fear the unknown and many people live under the impression that they know few or no disabled people. It is hard for non-disabled people to understand how someone can look like them but have a brain that functions so differently—unless the person's behavior is so markedly different that their disability again starts to become visible. Invisible disabilities remain largely just that—invisible. Practically speaking, it is pointless to be upset with people who misunderstand something they know little about and do not personally experience. I've always believed education was the appropriate response to ignorance.

I've also found that nothing changes a person's point of view on how disability of any kind can impacts a person's life like suddenly having personal experience. I've met more than one older professor who has come to have a whole new appreciation—and has adopted new teaching policies—following the diagnosis of a grandchild as being disabled. Once a person has intimate knowledge of how autism, for example, can lead to meltdowns, or ADD to difficulties tracking details, the formerly inexplicable behaviors that result from a condition suddenly are seen in a new light. Even those with experience with one disability however, often have limited experience with disability in general; they are willing, even eager to learn but they require a reliable source of information. I therefore will at this point dispel some of the prevalent myths that continue to circulate amongst faculty and staff on university campuses, in part because they are based on larger social myths which continue to be prevalent.

Anxiety disorder: everyone has it or no one has it

The biggest misinformation related to anxiety disorder grows from the practice of using similar words to mean very different things. Most educated people at some point have referred to themselves as "anxious" about an important event. Most people who cared enough about education to pursue it to the point of obtaining a degree have experienced nervousness about taking a test—they therefore believe they have had "test anxiety." I have yet to take part in a meeting or discussion about test anxiety without someone saying exactly that, "Everyone has test anxiety."

There is considerable difference between test anxiety and being nervous. There is an even greater distinction between having a larger anxiety disorder and having anxiety that is produced by testing situations, but for now we will focus on an anxiety attack that happens during a test. In Chapter Six I will go into much more detail about the group of mental illnesses which fall under the broader classification of anxiety disorders.

The symptoms of nervousness are:

- sweaty palms

- dry mouth

- looking flushed

- slightly elevated pulse/blood pressure

- difficulty staying physically still.

The symptoms of an anxiety attack are:

- chest pain that feels like a possible heart attack

- inability to draw full breaths

- inability to recall simple details

- full blown "flight response" as if facing a life or death situation.

When one is nervous, one can still begin to work one's way through a test, returning to questions that one may have to pass by during an initial read-through of the material. When one is having an anxiety, or panic attack, one will be unable to recall basic information that at other times one has full command of. A test given to a nervous person gives the tester an idea of what the person is learning. A test given to someone having an anxiety attack only begins to test how long the anxiety attack lasts in a test environment. I once had to turn in a test that had only my name on it because although I knew the information forward and backward in the days up to the test, once I was in the test environment I had an anxiety attack. Suddenly I was literally struggling to remember how to spell my name. By the time I turned in the test I couldn't have told my professor where I lived; I also couldn't speak to explain what had happened. I was reduced to mutely handing in my test and shrugging as the professor looked at me with wide-eyed surprise. I was not able to fill in any part of the test except my name.

Within about 20 minutes of leaving the testing environment, I was finally able to start breathing normally, made it successfully through some meditation and relaxation, and the information all came flooding back to me. If I'd had more practice doing these relaxation exercises during a test situation and if I'd had an accommodation for extended time, then I would have been able to successfully complete my exam.

It can be very difficult to tell the difference between a student who hasn't studied and one who has experienced a real anxiety attack during the exam. This is why students with anxiety disorders should be working with the disability service provider on campus and/or the counseling center.

QUICK FACTS

- The National Institute of Mental Health (NIMH) and National Health Services (NHS) amongst other leading medical organizations, recognize a related group of mental illnesses which fall under anxiety disorders and includes generalized anxiety disorder; obsessive compulsive disorder; panic disorder; post-traumatic stress disorder; social phobia.

- NIMH reports that a national study found that 8 percent of 13–18-year-olds suffer with an anxiety disorder (NIMH 2012a), while the NHS estimates that one in 20 adults in Britain have anxiety—with the disorder "most common" in people in their 20s (NHS 2012a).

- NIMH reports that two separate studies found differences in brain responses to "stress" stimuli between young people with anxiety disorder and those in the control groups—these were measurable differences in brain response to the same stimuli.

Anxiety disorder: tough it out and you will conquer your anxiety

Again, realizing that there is a significant difference between being nervous and having a form of anxiety disorder is paramount. We all tend to experience a level of nervousness when experiencing something unfamiliar for the first time—this is perfectly normal.

Having a reaction to events that is on the level of a disorder means that the person who is experiencing the event feels their life and wellbeing are threatened, often by "ordinary" events including meeting new people, having elements of their world out of order, or being placed in a test environment. Yes, most people are nervous in a crowd; only a small percentage of us, however, feel that the experience has the potential to cause us to run screaming, or to find a hiding place, or simply freeze up, unable to function. A condition becomes a "disorder" when it directly impacts a person's ability to function normally in day-to-day activities.

Once we understand that someone who has been diagnosed as having an anxiety disorder is, for reasons directly related to how his brain is responding to "normal" stimuli, unable to function in a normal fashion, we can begin to understand why continuing to experience the stimuli isn't going to *cure* the condition. There are some proponents of this "flooding" method, i.e. a person's ability to respond at all is so overwhelmed that they can be taught to mechanically respond to a limited extent in specific contexts. This is actually a method some dog trainers use, where they overwhelm a dog with something that the dog fears, until the dog ceases to respond. For example, when a dog barks at a skateboard, they continue to force the dog to encounter a skateboard until the dog becomes overwhelmed and ceases to bark. This is not training, however, it is simply breaking down the dog's ability to respond any further due to being overwhelmed.

While flooding may get a dog to stop barking at a specific stimulus, because the reactions we want from people are usually more complicated then ceasing to bark, flooding someone's mental circuitry with fear can seldom be followed up by gaining a desired response. In fact, we are more likely to have the opposite effect; the more we expose someone to stimuli which triggers an anxiety attack, the more likely their response is to deteriorate in the face of a particular stimulus. Many teachers have witnessed this in students whose fear surrounding performance grows during the semester; as the semester goes on the student's responses to tests or assigned writing continues to deteriorate. In the past it was usually assumed that this was a clear sign of a student not studying or working; it can also be an indication, however, of a student who is experiencing increasing incidents of anxiety disorder.

In Chapter Six I will discuss how providing low-risk opportunities to practice new knowledge/skills can help people work through anxiety that is triggered by events such as writing, test taking, and learning new jobs. I mention jobs not just because students with anxiety disorder can end up in work environments at university, but because it is important to realize that anxiety disorder is present not just in students, but also occurs in faculty and staff. As a result, administrators can improve a work environment and employee morale by also creating low-risk opportunities for those they supervise to learn, whether the learning is centered around a new pedagogical motivation for changing the design of a class, or a new computer program for processing information.

QUICK FACTS

- The Anxiety and Depression Association of America (ADAA) states that over 40 million people in the US live with anxiety and that only approximately one-third of these people are currently receiving treatment for their disorder (ADAA 2012).

- The results of a study of twins published in *JAMA* found that there was a genetic link in the development of depression and anxiety disorder, while environmental factors influenced the actual development of both disorders (Kendlar *et al*. 1992).

- Anxiety is often comorbid with other health problems; for example a US analysis of 2006 health reports found that anxiety disorder was present in 23 percent of people with asthma (Strine *et al*. 2008), while a German study found that over 18 percent of students from age 12–17 had a form of anxiety and that their anxiety was most often comorbid with depression (Essau *et al*. 2000).

Accommodations: extended time for tests can be an unfair advantage

This is such a common social myth that even disabled students have become entrenched in the idea that if they ask for the extended time they need to process information, they are asking for an unfair advantage over their peers. Because socially we have become more familiar in the past decade with visible disabilities, I sometimes find it helpful to reframe this conversation by comparing their invisible disability with a visible disability.

I will thus sometimes ask people, "Does a person who uses a wheelchair because they need it have an unfair advantage? What about a person who needs a guide dog and uses one?"

The two most common reasons that students are given extended test time both come back to physical differences in their brain vs. the "normal" brain that does not require extended test time.

1. The student has one of the range of language/processing disorders, so that their brain takes longer to processes the information that comes in or that is being output.

2. The student lives with one of the anxiety disorders which causes them to physically slow down due to a fearful/freezing reaction to stimuli present in a test environment.

Extended time is an attempt to allow the student to show what they know, as opposed to testing their reaction to a test environment or penalizing them for having slower language/processing mechanisms.

There are other reasons that extended time can be provided as an accommodation. I work with an increasing number of students who live with Crohn's disease and other forms of irritable bowel syndrome (IBS). Stress causes IBS to flare up, flare-ups lead to a person needing to rush to the lavatory, potentially repeatedly in a short period of time. As a result, a student with IBS, who is worried about running out of time on a test due to their IBS, is that much more likely to spend up to half their time in the lavatory, rather than writing their test. Again, extended test time helps reduce the student's level of stress and increase their opportunity to show the tester what they know, even though they may still need to use the lavatory during the exam. Due to an almost universal social norm that lavatories are dirty places and therefore not fit for discussion, students tend to be particularly embarrassed about disclosing this disability; they certainly do not want to discuss it more than absolutely necessary. I point this out because it impacts a related social myth—it is sometimes believed that students who choose not to discuss their disability do not really have a disability, or are trying to hide their disability when what they ought to be doing is disclosing to more people, at least their professors/supervisors.

Accommodations: I have to know exactly what a person's disability is in order to accurately accommodate him or her

Every year I work with professors and other professionals who insist they need to know what a person's actual disability is in order to provide the accommodations they have been told a person is entitled to. This is incorrect on a number of levels, two of which I will discuss here.

Personal dignity

Being disabled and wanting an education or employment no longer means a person has to give up all their personal dignity to everyone in the work place. We now have:

- laws that protect the rights of the disabled

- disability specialists who provide summaries of necessary accommodations.

As a disability specialist it is my job to review a person's documentation of a disability and to discern the accommodations that each individual requires. My colleague in Affirmative Programs works with employees at the university to provide a similar service. Our roles are to ensure what is reasonable and necessary accommodation. When we, as professionals, reach a decision and inform others of necessary accommodations, we have provided all the information that our colleagues in classrooms, administration, etc. are legally entitled to have.

It may be necessary to have further discussions with disability specialists about altering or providing the accommodations, conversations about who pays for which services, or how to interpret an accommodation. Neither supervisors nor professors, however, have either a legal or moral right to know exactly what an individual's disability is, unless the individual chooses to divulge that information without being pressured to do so. I for example, make it clear to the administrative assistants I work with that I am dyslexic and therefore I will require extra eyes and minds to help ensure I do not make obvious mistakes with scheduling dates, numbers, or names. I choose not to disclose other information about my disabilities with the majority of people I work with, as I do not want this information to color their perception of me and my work. My supervisor and I have discussed that even given the work I do, there is some information about some of my disabilities which could potentially make people hesitate to promote me or put me in certain positions in the work environment. Disclosure is always a very personal decision and may vary from context to context. What I choose to tell one person may not be something I choose to tell another. No one has the right to take this personal decision from the individual.

The law

As an employee of a post-secondary institution, an individual's actions can lay the institution open to law suits. Insisting someone disclose a disability or otherwise foregrounding disability in a way that makes one or more people in the work environment uncomfortable increases the likelihood that one is opening oneself and one's institution to a law suit. If one believes one needs more information in order to provide an accommodation, then one should have this discussion with the disability service provider; one should not try and pry private information from a student or employee.

QUICK FACTS

Most nations and the United Nations now provide legal protection for the rights of the disabled. I am including just a short, fairly random list of laws from around the globe; a fuller list of laws related to disabilities may be found at the website for Disability Rights Education and Defense Fund (DREDF 2007).

Australia—The Disability Discrimination Act of 1992.

Canada—Canadian Human Rights Act (1985).

Ecuador—Disabled Act (2001).

India—The Persons with Disabilities Act of 1995.

Japan—Basic Law on Persons with Disabilities (1970, amended 2004).

Korea—Welfare for Persons with Disabilities Act (WPWDA) 1989.

Malawi—Handicapped Persons Act, 1971.

New Zealand—Human Rights Act 1993.

UK—Equality Act of 2010, preceded by Disability Discrimination Act of 2005 (still in force in Northern Ireland).

UN—UN Convention on the Rights of Persons with Disabilities (169 signatory nations, UN, 2012).

US—Americans with Disabilities Act 1990.

Zambia—The Persons with Disabilities Act 1996.

Invisible disability means "easy to fake" *or* doctors will give you documentation for any invisible disability you claim you have

I suspect that several things feed into this myth. With the public perception that there has been a "rapid" increase in disabilities, there is a natural inclination to look for reasons: some people blame vaccines, some point to the increase of toxins in our environment, and some suspect that doctors now hand out disability diagnosis the way they used to hand out balloons or lollipops.

Studies have found no evidence to support the suspicion that vaccines can lead to disabilities. The World Health Organization reports just the opposite in fact (WHO 2008). Access to vaccinations can improve health and welfare, particularly amongst the poorest people in a nation who have limited access to healthcare.

Nor has there been as rapid an increase in the number of disabled people as is socially perceived; there have, however, been changes in how disorders are diagnosed, and diagnostically, what counts as a disorder. Let us consider what is now recognized as a spectrum of disorders—autism. It is impossible to measure how much of an actual increase there has been in the incident of autism because the diagnostic criteria for autism has changed so significantly since first being described in the 1940s. This will be explained in more detail in Chapter Three. As an example, though, my father did his training in special education in the late 1960s. He recalls that at that time there were five specific criteria that a child had to meet in order to be diagnosed as autistic and that these criteria included an unwillingness to be touched, rocking behavior, self-harm—behaviors which now are seen as being just a small part of the spectrum of behavior that an autistic child may display. This was before higher functioning autism like Asperger's was recognized as part of the autism spectrum and when we still labeled some people "idiot savants"—people who are now recognized as also being on the autism spectrum, and are currently called "autistic savants." So while the number of people diagnosed as being on the autism spectrum has increased, this is in part the result of diagnostic criteria changing over the years and only partially an increase of the actual incident of the disorder; the numbers have not grown as dramatically and quickly as statistics suggest.

At the same time, environmental factors are undoubtedly playing a role in some increase in incidents of disorder. While the *New York Times* article, "Father's age is linked to risk of autism and schizophrenia" (Carey 2012) made much of a portion of an Icelandic study that found more mutations in the genetic material of "older fathers" (ignoring that older in this case meant 33 years of age) the *Times* did not report a very significant fact that was contained in the original study. The Icelandic researchers reported that, "There has been a recent transition of Icelanders from a rural agricultural to an urban industrial way of life" (Kong *et al.* p.474). The researchers also point out that traditionally (at least since 1900) fathers in Iceland had been about 34 years of age, but that this changed from approximately 1980 until 2011, when the average father's age dropped to 27, before suddenly climbing back up to 33—the researchers suggest this sudden reversal was, "primarily owing to the effect of higher education and the increased use of contraception" (Kong *et al.* p.474). I would suggest that the original Icelandic study was showing a correlation between aging, exposure to industrial environments, and increased incidents of genetic mutation. These factors seem to work together; the older a father, the more environmental exposure he will have received and there is an increased likelihood that his DNA will be genetically mutated, thus impacting the children he sires. Remember, it is harder to compare pre-1980 autistic incidents to post-2011 numbers due to a change in diagnostic criteria over that span of time. What can be shown is that from 1980 until the end of the study, incidents of DNA mutation have increased, as have the number of people moving from rural settings to urban.

As for doctors over-diagnosing disabilities—studies tend to show just the opposite. As mentioned previously, bipolar disorder often takes ten years to be correctly diagnosed, with people suffering without adequate treatment in the interim. In order for a learning disability to be diagnosed a person must take a range of tests—testing can be spread over several days—and the results of tests are compared to look for a reoccurring pattern of strengths and weaknesses which indicate a disability is present. For example, multiple tests can be used which reinforce the result that a person has an average or high intelligence, and functions very well in all areas, with the exception of a particular area such as processing written words, or an ability to mentally manipulate a two-dimensional figure. This is an indication that a particular function of the brain is impaired. Tests can be given which indicate the exact functioning areas that are impaired and suggestions can then be made by the specialists conducting the testing on ways the student can be accommodated. Given the battery of tests needed to prove a disability to the specialists who do this testing, it is anything but easy to consistently fake the same disability across the range of tests given.

This is a separate matter from the writing of prescriptions for medication to support students who talk to their family doctor about anxiousness, depression, inability to focus, etc. I have personally witnessed students receiving prescriptions for medications without having the corresponding battery of tests to "prove" their disability. It is a matter of opinion and speculation regarding if/when this is ever appropriate, given that some people do clearly display all the indications of a disability without being able to afford the specialized testing necessary to prove such a disability. I will not speculate about how frequently this practice occurs.

I will state that disability service providers look to written reports by the appropriate specialists when seeking documentation for a disability; handing a disability service provider a copy of one's prescription is not considered valid documentation by any service provider I am aware of, or whose written policies I have encountered (and I have spent considerable time looking at online policies from a range of post-secondary institutions.) Again, what is much more common is for universities to try and place a burden on students to prove their disability that is so cumbersome that governments have made legislative changes to reduce this burden on the individual who seeks an education. The 2010 revisions to the *Americans with Disabilities Act* is an example of this legislative clarification of what is considered reasonable documentation, while also limiting an institution's and individual's previously perceived rights-to-question the disabled person.

In the chapters which follow I will go into greater detail about specific groups of disabilities, including providing a synopsis of how diagnosis is typically arrived at and the most common accommodations which can support the learning of a person within each group of disabilities. I believe that with education and explanation, there will come greater understanding of why people in learning environments require the different kinds of supports they are being given. I also have seen that when professors and staff have a better understanding of the brain processes going on behind the label of a disability, the more likely they are to have new ideas for how to assist in providing learning support. My personal experience in post-secondary institutions has been that most people are very willing to participate in supporting the learning and lives of disabled people—what they lack in doing so is an understanding of how to achieve this goal.

Some readers may choose at this point to skip directly to Chapter Three where I begin the discussion of specific disabilities. Chapter Two will take a closer look at how the roles of teaching and administration will by default have to change in the face of our changing students, if for no other reason than because as our countries' legislation changes, increasing emphasis will be placed on education being accessible to all. This has not traditionally been the practice; the longer standing tradition is that education is for an elite few and this remains more the standard than the exception. Disabilities, however, are now acknowledged to fall across the socioeconomic spectrum and as a result, families of privilege are just as likely to produce disabled children as families of the poor. The elite continue to demand education for their young and increasingly often these young may be autistic, ADD, dyslexic, or mentally ill. Socially, however, these young people are no longer expected to be hidden from the rest of society. These facts will change how we in universities are required to do our work.

CHAPTER TWO

How Legalities and New Students Will Change Post-Secondary Work

There was no easing into our most recent fall semester. I talked to a number of colleagues, both at the institution where I work and from institutions around the country. We were all noticing that student stress levels were at higher levels early in the semester. When I first began teaching at the post-secondary level, students actually seemed to enjoy the first semester of school. That gradually changed to enjoying the first half of the semester—most recently, there was no perceived period of enjoyment of being newly independent. Everyone seemed to hit the ground during orientation week, already prepared to self-combust from a combination of stress, nerves, and mild to severe depression.

This environment takes a toll not just on students, but also on those of us who work with them. When one sees a steady stream of underprepared students it quickly becomes discouraging, disheartening, and somewhat exhausting. As a teacher I find it much easier to work with a class where students bring in some positive energy, and tiring when trying to overcome a negative energy present among the members of the class. As an administrator, dealing with a parade of overwhelmed people leaves me exhausted by the end of the day. While the level of anxiousness among students suggests my role is more than ever necessary, my energy for doing the work is more quickly depleted in the face of so much negativity. It seems impossible for anyone who works in post-secondary education to be removed from the impact of the increasing number of distressed students.

Disability is only one source of stress

Our commerce is increasingly impacted by global events. As a result, none of us has been immune from some stress related to changes in markets, recessions, technological changes to types of employment, and redistribution of demands for labor. People increasingly have to move geographically to find work and from one field of expertize to another in order to maintain employment. Perhaps because we have come to expect more than a paycheck from our employment, there also seems to be an increasing amount of unhappiness with work environments in general. In reading responses to an online article, "6 reasons to make a career change" (McKay 2013), I was struck by the fact that all 29 people who responded to the article shared stories of unhappiness with their work environment. Once upon a time it was commonplace to spend one's entire career with an employer; not only does this happen infrequently now, it seems many people are demoralized by the idea of having to remain with their current employer at all and would change jobs immediately if they had the opportunity.

There also seems to be an increasing number of employers so quick to assume that people will eventually leave their employment that they do not perceive that constant staff turnover can be a sign of legitimate complaints with the work environment. Employers also seem to undervalue the people filling jobs that do not require as much education, apparently oblivious to their own lost investment in training and employee-retained knowledge when employees leave a job and new people have to be found and trained. The abundance of applicants for open jobs seems to blind employers to the cost of interviewing, training, and offering trial periods to new people. The University of Northern Iowa's *Executive Development Center* featured a blog post, "The true cost of replacing an employee" which points out that it costs "about $3500 to replace one $8.00 per hour employee" while a company will spend between $20,000–$60,000 to bring a hired person making $40,000 a year up to speed and trained to do their job (Recker 2012).

Ross Blake, in his online article "Employee retention: what employee turnover really costs your company" says that it is remarkably common for employers to underestimate the cost of replacing employees or to not be proactive about keeping valuable employees (Blake 2006). Blake explains that he frequently encounters managers who believe that as long as an employee is not threatening to quit, then there do not need to be specific measures taken to address employee dissatisfaction. Even when managers are aware that strongly performing employees are unhappy, they will often turn a blind eye until the employee is ready to quit. According to Blake very few companies track the cost of replacing employees, and even if someone does track this information they seldom consider *all* the components of cost; even if accurately estimated the final numbers seldom get passed on to top management so that they are aware of the cost the business is incurring due to employee turnover.

People appear less happy in their work at least in part because employers seem less concerned about employee turnover even though this makes poor business sense. Post-secondary institutions are not in a magic bubble that protects them from these trends. Professors and administrators are increasingly mobile among campuses as they seek "better" fits for their personal and professional goals. Those who are less mobile often find themselves mired in negative, demoralized work atmospheres. Is it any wonder then, that as we work with increasingly stressed students worried about their grades, their financial investment, and their opportunities, we all find ourselves edgier and feeling more frazzled. Every week *The Chronicle of Higher Education* seems to have a new story in which a faculty member laments the devaluing of education in general and specifically a new example they have witnessed of knowledge for knowledge's sake being dismissed as valueless. To summarize, the lament seems to be, "No one wants to learn, everyone just wants to get a job that pays well." Seen from this point of view, it is easy to see why faculty and staff groan at the thought of one more layer of demands and burdens being placed on them as they must increasingly change standard operating procedures to accommodate disabled students and colleagues.

Ironically, as one group is moved towards greater equality and justice, other groups who must make changes begin to feel they are being unfairly burdened. Every time there is a shift in social procedures there will be ripple effects. When institutions were told that they needed to allow women, minorities, students from lower socioeconomic groups, non-native language speakers—any previously excluded group in—there were adjustments and changes needed throughout the institutions. Schools incurred costs when they had to build dormitories and physical education spaces for women; when they recognized a need to institute "entry level" education for students who were no longer similarly prepared to begin university; when they had to modify their campuses to make them physically accessible. Accommodating the increasing number of invisibly disabled students will also not be without financial and emotional costs. From the point of view of the disabled students, they no longer have to bear all these costs alone, as society recognizes that there is value to be gained from including one more group of previously excluded people in the higher education process.

It is time for all of us—faculty and staff—to disabuse ourselves, however, of the notion that we are not personally going to have to bear some of these costs in our own work life. There was a time when being a professor meant suddenly having to adjust to women/minorities/the poor/the physically disabled in the classroom; when administrators were suddenly faced with a host of new students they had no experience dealing with. Such times continue to be upon us. Rather than insisting that one will not take part in this process (one's only real option at this point is to find another line of work) it is more realistic to consider this reality in negotiating the demands on one's time and the compensation one will receive for this work. The best time to do this is when accepting a new job—part of negotiating a post-secondary position these days should include taking into account the amount of time one will be required to spend preparing and supplying accommodations for disabled students and/or supervisees. Clarify with a potential employer what they will expect and what support they will offer in regard to providing accommodations. In order to facilitate this conversation I will now outline some of the changes that can logically be expected in post-secondary education in the foreseeable future; one may need to use some of these points as a foundation for a dialogue with specific examples when negotiating the expectations of new employment or a promotion.

More time for testing; more versions of a test?

In the discussions of different groups of disabilities which will follow, it will become increasingly clear why I state emphatically at this point that there will be an increase, not decrease, in both the number of students requiring extended test time and a need for professors to be more flexible regarding the actual time when a student will write a test. Professors and administrators will serve their own interests best if they immediately begin planning for flexibility for a range of testing times. It will also be necessary to have more than one test environment—unless that one environment is made up of multiple, individual, soundproof spaces; not everyone will need such spaces, however, some students absolutely will.

Policies to be discussed/decided on individual campuses will include:

- where will the physically accessible test space be located

- who will be responsible for staffing the space (consider that adjuncts/instructors will not have the flexibility of time/resources that a tenured professor with a TA will have)

- who will be responsible for maintaining the space

- who will pay for the supplies used within the space.

Fortunately for many institutions, they have already had this initial conversation and have a centralized test-center which meets the majority of the campus' testing needs. Unfortunate are the campuses such as the one where I currently work, who are still facing the growing pains that will include resolving many of these issues. Many institutions will, however, still need to reflect on the capacity of the current spaces they are using and may need to begin planning for expanded demand on these spaces. Unfortunately, the way testing typically works, there are peak times when the demand for space is greatest, meaning that with an increasing number of students requiring the space, there will be more need and thus more space required.

While many of the policy decisions will involve administrators, faculty and departments would benefit from discussions and adopting policy statements which clarify for students:

- How much notice the student needs to provide faculty to receive test accommodations.

- Whether the professors' preferred way of receiving notice of a right to accommodation is in keeping with federal law/university policy (is the professor requesting notice in a format that is not standard? I have witnessed this, so I consider it a necessary part of the conversation).

- Storage and management of a central data-base of questions for tests which may require multiple versions if a department/professor does not wish to give the same version of a test at different times.

During a recent discussion with one department on campus I was struggling to clarify with the department faculty how we were going to proctor the increasing number of extended time tests necessary within the department. One of the professors suddenly realized a simple and elegant solution; if the department designed all their tests to be completed within 50 minutes, announced this fact in their syllabi and classes, then scheduled rooms and supervisors so that all students would have two hours to write the exam, they would have (a) provided everyone with double time for the exam (meeting federal/ university standards); (b) eliminated the need for much of their outside proctoring for their students. This is an example of what is called "universal design"—the idea that when we plan from the point of view of accommodating everyone at the same time, we can eliminate perceived difficulties that are actually only present in our "traditional" way of doing things. In Chapters Eight and Nine more examples of universal design will be presented.

Sorry but spelling and grammar cannot always count

If a professor/instructor requires students to keep written journals, to compose in-class writing which needs to be turned in, or gives essay tests that are not on a computer with spell-check—then poor and even "slovenly" handwriting, grammar, and spelling will increasingly have to be accommodated. Some who teach will already have adjusted to this need to accommodate language processing and other disorders affecting reading/writing by allowing students with the appropriate accommodations to use computers in-class and for exams. Others may choose to move towards more oral examination of students with particularly severe language processing disorders.

I have heard faculty and staff voice the concern that anyone who has such a significant language processing disorder that he or she is unable to write out an exam certainly cannot have any real future in… [fill in any career field you can think of]. Several points.

1. The governments of the world are in increasing agreement that it is a university's job to educate and the workplace's role to discern who is actually qualified for doing a job.

2. People will continue to defy expectations and prove successful in fields one would not predict, just as people who are predicted to be successful will continue on occasion to have spectacular failures.

Correct or not, there is a social impression that universities have too long been gate-keepers and are too removed from the "real world" to judge accurately which students will prove to be successful in a job upon graduation. This does not mean, in my opinion, that faculty cannot provide opinions when asked by a student to do so. If a student in one's field of major asks for your factual perception of the strengths and limitations that they as an individual will bring to the field, then a factual assessment is in order. Deciding that it is one's individual place, however, to weed out a student is not appropriate. Individual opinions are too likely to be influenced by personal bias and experience. No one person's experience is universally representative of all possible experiences within a field. I personally have been enrolled in classes with professors who thought I had no business pursuing study; these professors believed my challenges with reading and writing were predictors of my future failure. I will be the first to admit, it did take me longer to learn some forms of academic writing than it takes some people—no one who doubted my capacity, though, realized how much time and effort I was willing to put into the endeavor.

Realize also, that an individual's disability or capacities *may* provide obstacles that will prevent that individual from being successful *working* in a specific field—and that the individual *may still choose* to follow the line of study for reasons of personal development and growth. Also realize that disabled students have the same right as able-bodied people to make poor choices. If one has ever watched an elimination round for a talent contest, one will realize that people pursue dreams in denial of their lack of talent or capacity for interests they are passionate about. Just as a talent scout can turn down an act but not stop someone from continuing to perform, as individuals within an academic institution what we can do is grade responses and set standards for performance. We are not allowed to unilaterally decide who should be allowed to try—our decisions must be made based on standard policies that are applied evenly to all students. Institutions and the individuals they employ need to disabuse themselves of the notion that it is their "job" to stop people short of spending time and money studying an interest that they have only moderate talent for; we can provide a standard set of policies, including requiring minimum GPAs, and enforce these policies uniformly.

In the work environment

If a disability is present in the wider social spectrum, then it will almost always be present amongst the faculty and staff who work in post-secondary education. I have worked with employees who have great potential that was not initially recognized because their language processing disabilities caused them to be mistaken for lazy or less intelligent. We are beyond the point socially when it is safe to assume that sloppy handwriting, or difficulty spelling/reading are the signs of either lack of education or lack of interest in one's work. One may wonder, "Well, when would anyone be asked to read/write outside of what is strictly for work purposes." My response: departmental retreats and performance reviews.

Post-secondary education is resplendent with seminars, retreats, and continuing education opportunities that have the potential to place those of us with language processing disorders in very embarrassing positions. I have lost track of the number of times I have been asked to take part in small group work in such a situation, then been told I either need to read something out to the larger group, or write a chart to place on the wall for others to view. My colleagues know that I am educated, so I think they sometimes assume I must just be lazy or careless in such circumstances, due to my inability to spell and my rather weak handwriting. If I have to read unfamiliar material out loud I am likely to verbally stumble. I feel a little uncomfortable in these contexts. I find these contexts discriminatory for my invisibly disabled peers who have not had the advantage of advanced degrees and whose handwriting, spelling, and grammar errors are mistaken for a lack of intelligence or an example of a poor education. Universal design has a place in designing such events, just as it has in the classroom. Events can be set up so that a range of ways of showing knowledge and idea processing are possible, rather than the academic impulse to turn every event into a reading and writing contest.

Employees are also sometimes judged on performance reviews, where they are required to write out an explanation of the work they do. Yet a performance review is not something people are traditionally trained in preparing, or have mentored opportunities to practice. As a result, those with invisible disabilities may be judged by supervisors and human resources as being lacking in intelligence, education, or an understanding of their work simply because they do not write out a performance review the way a supervisor implicitly expects the review to be written. I have worked with employees who have been denied raises because they did not fill out their performance reviews the way supervisors expected them to. The issue came down to difference in expectations for how to write these reviews, and invisible disabilities impacting a person's writing.

Disabled students are not more responsible than other students

I've noticed a trend among disabled students: they tend to fall at one of two points on a spectrum. They tend to either be very well-organized and have developed useful strategies for success, which is how they made it to university or, they tend to have relied for so long on their superior intellect that they have developed virtually no practical skills for self-organization and responsibility. Of course, there are some who fall in-between these extremes, but they do seem to be in the minority.

My point is that based on meeting some of the well-organized disabled students, one may expect all disabled students to be capable of being organized and responsible. It is hard to appreciate the dichotomy of the student who is very intelligent yet has a disability which makes organizing, handing in work, or keeping track of simple things nearly impossible. It often appears that if a person is "that smart" and yet can't hand in their homework, they must not really care about a class; or if they are "that charming" yet can't arrive to work on time they must be trying to take advantage of their supervisor/co-workers. In the sections which follow I will clarify how brains differently organize information so that it becomes clearer how the executive functioning needed to do a perfect job on homework does not particularly overlap with the functioning needed to manage dates/times, or that being sincere and charismatic works out of a different portion of the brain than the ability to track and judge time.

Faculty and staff can adapt techniques that will provide better support for students who lack certain executive functions or who need practice making better use of some of these functions. My own research has found that people learn new things best when they have had the opportunity for hands-on practice; it is possible to provide hands-on practice with handing work in or keeping schedules. I will discuss these points further in Chapters Eight and Nine.

Both teachers and administrators would benefit from a little more insight into why being very good in one area of information processing while having a deficit in another is the very hallmark of disability. The larger question at this point may be, how does this knowledge impact my work?

- At least initially, more time will be needed to universally design class activities, spaces, and workloads so that employees' strengths are utilized and students have an opportunity to show what they know.

- Increasing use of user testing of "new ways of doing" will decrease frustration with policies and practices which otherwise might overlook the impact they have on the disabled, e.g. a language-heavy form will discriminate against those with language processing disorders (discussion to be found in Chapter Nine).

- By implementing universal design throughout an institution, both employee and student retention can be increased—saving or generating more income results from increased retention of staff and students.

- Disability is an aspect of diversity—diverse ideas, viewpoints, and opinions result from including the invisibly disabled in designing and adapting policy and procedures (discussion to be found in Chapter Ten).

If we do not prepare to give diverse, disabled people the same rights and respect that we have previously given other disenfranchised groups, then as in the past these rights will be (and are being increasingly) demanded. As stated earlier in this chapter—if working with the invisibly disabled proves too problematic for an individual in administration or teaching, then it is time for that person to be educating him or herself towards a new career. There is less tolerance on federal legal levels for forms of discrimination which were allowed in the past.

For example, it used to be considered "normal" to demand a student explain what their disability was to a range of individuals at the institution every time a new request for accommodation was made—in housing, in dining halls, classrooms, etc. This is no longer legal or justified. When there are questions that need answering regarding a person's eligibility for services, the disability service provider on campus is the person to communicate with and that person will most likely clarify your duties and obligations, not give you in-depth information about an individual's specific disability. *It is legitimate* to ask the disability service provider, or one's supervisor, for an explanation of how to achieve an accommodation; it is not legal or necessary to know what disability in particular causes a person to require the accommodation they require. The right to disclose a disability or the specifics of a disability remain with the disabled individual, not the institution or the disability service provider.

CHAPTER THREE

Autism Spectrum Disorders, Including Asperger's Syndrome

Diagnostic and Statistical Manual of Mental Disorders, Fifth Edition—(DSM-V) has modified the definition of autism spectrum disorder, to include what used to be referred to as Asperger's syndrome; individuals may continue to self-refer to themselves as having Asperger's, as this indicates that they are "high-functioning" compared to some individuals living with autism spectrum disorder (ASD). Indicators of ASD include:

- challenges with social communication and interactions
- difficulty in understanding and maintaining relationships
- inability or struggle to read body language and facial expressions
- repeating behaviors
- hypo- or hypersensitivity to pain, temperature and other sensory input
- limited, focused interests
- hypersensitivity to small changes.

ASD students who arrive at college are often very intelligent. They are more drawn to science, technology, engineering, math, and computer fields. They may demonstrate little or no flexibilty; their comments may appear out of context or disruptive. These are the students with such specialized interests and knowledge that they will correct professors when they feel an inaccurate statement has been made, both because they prefer accurate, factual information and because they are blind to the social inappropriateness of students correcting professors in front of a class.

Background

Mental health disturbances and differences between types of disturbances, were gaining increased attention at the turn of the 20th century. In the 1930s, schizophrenia was just being recognized as a particular strand of mental illness; shortly after doctors began to recognize schizophrenia in adults, there grew a debate about whether or not there was ever childhood onset of the disease. In 1943 Leo Kanner announced that based on his studies he found that most often children were suffering from a separate disorder—he referred to this disorder as "early infantile autism" with the word finding its root in the word "auto" to indicate that child has interest in only self; this is now defined as classic autism (Bursztyn 2007, p.7). An autistic infant is not interested in interacting with others and may actually seem repulsed by a parent's touch. The toddler will be withdrawn and display repetitive actions; as a child grows he or she will continue to display little communication ability and usually appear uninterested in the people around them. These children seem locked inside themselves. I remember as a young person hearing adults speak of autistic children as being perfect examples of "living in a world by themselves." They meant that each child was locked in an individual world, where there was little or no communication with anyone outside him or herself.

One of the reasons that the statistical number of children affected with autism has grown so much since autism was first described in 1943 is that we now recognize that this "classic autism" is just one point on a spectrum of autistic disorders—or ASD—autism spectrum disorders. Just as we know that schizophrenia was present in the general population before it was medically recognized, defined, and named, we know that ASD was present—we therefore cannot accurately judge if the number of affected children has increased dramatically or otherwise. We do now know that autism takes more forms than the one Kanner first described. In fact, at the university level we are most likely to encounter what is considered "the other end of the spectrum" from classic autism: Asperger's syndrome.

Originally described in a journal article in 1944 by Hans Asperger, Asperger himself labeled the disorder "autistic psychopathy" a name which was later changed due to the negative association the term "psychopathy" had taken on. In 1981 Lorna Wing originally suggested this change, which was then adopted and further popularized by Uta Frith in a 1991 publication (Frith 1991; Wing 1998; Baron-Cohen and Klin 2006). In her discussions of Asperger's work, Wing has pointed out that while Asperger did not provide rigid diagnostic criteria, he did provide signposts of the disorder (which are still considered diagnostically relevant and can often be observed as one becomes familiar with an individual who lives with Asperger's.) To paraphrase Wing/Asperger, the indicators include:

- Children who appear naive, are very sensory aware, and "emotionally detached."

- While unaware of others' feelings, they are themselves hyper-sensitive to criticism.

- Grammatically fluent but interested in tyrannical speech/ monologues, not dialogues.

- Odd speech inflection or lack of inflection.

- Tendency towards very specialized interests, at times to an obsessive level.

Group identity

As a group, those who live with Asperger's often refer to themselves as "Aspies" and refer to those who are not on the ASD spectrum as "neuro-typical" (NT). One can gain insights into how Aspies represent themselves by observing posts on popular media sites such as YouTube, which allow people to post videos they have created with their personal technology, such as a home computer with webcam. Spending some time viewing these videos, one can also begin to develop a sense of conflicts that are taking place within the community, including concerns about who has the right to speak about the experience of being autistic. At the same time, neuro-typical family members do want to be part of the support community and at times do speak out about how autism affects the wider community; it can be educational to spend time viewing the range of opinions about where support ends and where speaking to someone else's experience begins. As with so many issues surrounding the autistic community, who can speak on their behalf and to what extent is a controversial and complex topic. "Authorities" are to some extent limited to providing data, guidelines, and suggestions. It is also important to remember something that is considered general wisdom by those who do work and live with those on the autistic spectrum: "If you've met one autistic person, then you've met one autistic person." The point being that as a spectrum disorder, how individuals are impacted varies widely and one person's lived experience of the disorder is not necessarily similar to another person's.

It is helpful for those who are not part of the autistic community to realize that being autistic is generally not viewed as a negative by those who are part of the community, particularly when they live with Asperger's (Shore 2003; Willey 1999). As with every disability, what is limiting for an individual are the contexts society places them in, not the disability in and of itself. Disabilities themselves are not what handicap a person; contexts create handicaps.

This may seem counterintuitive, so let us conduct a thought experiment. Imagine that the only way one could get from one level of a building to another, was to go outside and climb a steep ladder. That context would handicap a number of people. Now let us imagine that it is windy, cold, and raining so that the ladder is icing up—even more people are handicapped from reaching higher floors. Suppose one does reach the fifth floor of a building, by ladder, and then someone takes the ladder away—suddenly everyone is handicapped and unable to leave the fifth floor without risking injury or death. How our buildings, social contexts, etc. are designed and set up are what handicap people, not their actual disability. *We design buildings the way we do to accommodate the average person, which handicaps those who fall outside the average.* A blind person who is physically fit would do better on a ladder climbing from meeting to meeting, than would a sighted person who spends the majority of their time sedentary on the ground level, if both are suddenly required to climb to the third floor for a meeting.

With autism, what handicaps the individual are contexts that tend to put emphasis on social interactions in rooms with poor ventilation, industrial lighting and odors, where sound often reverberates off walls, or where it is easier to hear the person whispering a few seats over, than the professor talking at the front of a lecture hall. People with Asperger's are not intellectually wanting, in fact, they are often the smartest people in the room. They can be handicapped, however, by a strong emphasis being placed on social interactions that they are not well-equipped to deal with, in environments that they find physically uncomfortable. Many students find classrooms uncomfortable, with fluorescent lighting that tends to increase the incidence of headaches, chairs that are one-size-fits-all, and professors who may speak too low/in monotones/or take the long way around to making a point. When one is born autistic, the probability that these factors will be handicapping are dramatically increased.

Physiology

In the *Current Opinion in Neurobiology* article, "Brainstem, cerebellar and limbic neuroanatomical abnormalities in autism," it was reported that autopsy studies have found that those with autism actually have more densely packed neuro-transmitters in key areas of the brain responsible for stimuli reception and transmission (Courchesne 1997). This explains why students with autism often find lights, smells, sounds, more overwhelming—the lights are brighter, the smells stronger, the sounds louder for them because their brains create greater response to sensory stimuli.

Current Opinion in Neurology carried the article, "Contributions of the environment and environmentally vulnerable physiology to autism spectrum disorders," which concludes that there is evidence now to suggest that environmental factors are contributing to triggering autism, particularly in those who have a genetic predisposition for the disorder (Herbert 2010). This finding was further supported by the Icelandic study so widely reported by the *New York Times*, that fathers who have been exposed to more environmental factors and greater genetic (de-novo) mutations, are more likely to sire autistic children (Carey 2012; Kong *et al.* 2012). This research leads to the observation that as an increasingly educated population waits to have children, while also migrating to urban centers in larger numbers, the incidence of autism spectrum disorders will continue to rise in the near future. In turn, educators and administrators will see the number of affected students also continue to rise as a new generation enters the educational system. The number of autistic students is not likely to stabilize in the near future, which means that the sooner a school begins to build accommodations into their systems, i.e. to universally design spaces, curriculum, and expectations, the better prepared they will be for the students who will arrive in the years to come.

Comorbid disorders

Autism spectrum disorder is often comorbid with other disorders, that is, an individual is usually also living with other disorders in addition to autism. Autism is so often found to be comorbid with other disorders that the University of Gothenburg, Sweden, conducted a study "To provide a clinically useful analysis of the extent," of coexistence of other medical conditions (Gillberg and Billstedt 2000, p.321). The findings conclude that it should be "expected" to find autism comorbid with other disorders. What might surprise people not familiar with autism are the range and types of comorbid disorders, including eating disorders (including anorexia, pica, and hoarding food), abnormal sleep patterns, and self-harm, including knuckle biting, hair pulling, and hitting themselves. The researchers made an interesting observation at the close of their article, "The realization that autism is not a [sic] often encountered in the shape of a 'pure' disorder, which one can easily separate out from all other conditions, should make obvious the need of new approaches in research" (Gillberg and Billstedt, p.328). This is an important factor for educators and administrators to realize as well—when accommodating students with autism, we are seldom accommodating just autism.

In the student population I currently work with, autism is often comorbid with at least one and sometimes all of the following: attention deficit/hyperactive disorder, dyslexia, depression, obsessive compulsive disorder, bipolar disorder, and anxiety disorder. In fact, autism in and of itself is not something we generally can accommodate—we focus instead on accommodating the coexisting disorders and when possible, provide social support for students to help them learn to manage the impact that autism has on their social interactions.

Presentation

We are seldom conscious of our own abilities to perceive what other people are likely to be thinking based on their facial expression, however, such capacity for what is referred to as "mind reading" based on facial cues is ordinary. This is one area where autism directly impacts the capacity a person has for social interactions; studies show that autism impairs or removes the capacity for "mind reading" (Baron-Cohen *et al.* 1997). An inability to perceive the mental state of others directly impacts a person's capacity for empathy. When one cannot perceive that others are experiencing internal mental states, one cannot experience the sense of sharing ideas or feelings with others. Unable to make this kind of connection with other people, those living with autism are destined to remain emotionally isolated. People who live with autism have emotions; they are not able to judge what emotions or ideas are being triggered in others, even as they may be saying or doing things which dramatically impact the people they are interacting with.

As a result, they are often perceived by others as being emotionally cold or indifferent, and are even accused of lacking a sense of humor. This of course is not usually true (any individual is capable of having a limited sense of humor). Particularly for those living with Asperger's, though, humor is often a reaction to something that is intellectually stimulating, ideas that are amusing, as opposed to "sight gags" which may elicit a laugh from others. Watching someone get hit in the face with a board would not usually be funny; a rabbit that is also a deadly monster is humorous because it juxtaposes the ideas of soft and cuddly with ferocious, creating an ironic statement.

Similarly, just like other human beings, those living with autism wish to be part of social groups and have friendships. They are handicapped by the social expectation that relationships include reciprocal sharing of feelings. Individuals and groups need to be able to accept someone who is not perceptive of the emotions or ideas of others in order to be inclusive of those who are autistic. Becoming friends with someone on the spectrum may push an individual's ability to accept someone exactly as they are; friendship for those on the spectrum is one more routine they would like to develop and maintain for a lifetime. While someone on the spectrum may not automatically know how a friend is feeling, they will memorize a friend's preferences and both value and give loyalty. If one shares an interest with someone on the spectrum, then one has a friend who will never grow tired or bored discussing this interest. Those on the spectrum are also open to fairly blunt explanations of what is and is not socially accepted behavior; they seldom expect to understand why these social rules are in place. As group members, spectrum students will often offer unique perspectives and think of details that others overlook. Spectrum students also are able to bring painstaking attention to detail to tasks they are engaged in; finding a way to engage such active minds can be a welcome challenge to teachers who enjoy a student who can become fascinated in detail about a topic.

Administratively, it helps to understand that spectrum students tend to be literalists, who perceive rules and regulations as very valuable guides. These are students who usually want more rules, not fewer, because they want expectations clarified to the greatest extent possible, with as little deviation for personal interpretation as possible. This means when a spectrum student believes an individual or institution is not following their own policies, they will quickly become agitated and usually demand explanations, or changes. Consistency is very important because routine helps make up for what appears to be emotional randomness on the part of those surrounding a student, e.g., people appear to react unpredictably but rules provide steadfast guidelines. While a spectrum student cannot "guess" why people do most of the things they do, rules help provide a foundation on which relationships can develop. Teachers have specific roles and leadership is usually respected—unless it appears to be fuzzy, illogical, poorly organized and thus frustrating and even harder to understand. When a spectrum student is frustrated by what strikes them as haphazardness and lack of organization and knowledge, they will usually appear to speak down to the person who they perceive to be incapable of performing their role within an institution (or classroom, including fellow students.)

Support

Structure is incredibly important for spectrum students. Of course, not all events can be predicted and run according to a schedule; however, it is important to recognize that in any group of students one is working with, at least some of those students will find the expectation to be spontaneous overwhelming. (Chapters Eight and Nine will discuss universal design and incorporating consideration of student differences in the lecture hall and smaller classes.)

When possible, providing outlines, schedules, and explicit instructions for tasks is useful—spectrum students cannot be expected to intuit what one expects of them and they will never "just know" what other students seem to know. And while this is a population that values clear guidelines, do not expect these students to find policies on their own; while a few individuals will know in exacting detail what the policies are, others will need reminders of what is written in handbooks, syllabi, or online. Remember, many spectrum students are also living with attention deficit or language processing disorders which means obtaining and processing information can be additional challenges they face.

Spectrum students can be overly sensitive to sensory input including lights, smells, and sounds. Ironically, some spectrum students can be very oblivious to their personal odor and the loudness of their own voice. Spectrum students sometimes create public scenes which embarrass professors, staff, or fellow students by speaking too loudly for a context, and saying things that are considered socially inappropriate. One example that springs to mind is a spectrum student matter-of-factly telling a fellow student that the sudden death of the student's parents meant he would have more free time without social obligations. Other students believed he said this to be cruel, while the autistic student was actually trying to be helpful, pointing out what struck him as a "silver lining" to the situation.

Others have found themselves feeling intimidated by a spectrum student's loud voice, which can rise as the spectrum student feels increasing distress. Again, while the student perceives their own emotional distress, they do not perceive that their reaction is upsetting to others. "Meltdowns" may appear threatening when in fact, the person having the meltdown simply lacks a more appropriate way to deal with their distress. Spectrum students do tend to respond well to a matter-of-fact explanation of how their response has been inappropriate, followed by an explanation of what the appropriate responses in a given context are, i.e. "If you wish to discuss this grade, you must write down your reasons for thinking this grade should be different, then you must send me that written response so that I can read it and respond to your points." Pointing out the most logical approach to a situation always works well with college students who are autistic—they understand logic in a way they can never understand the emotions of others.

Public figures

It is sometimes helpful to put a public face to a disorder, in part to point out that the disorder does not preclude people from accomplishing success in a variety of fields. While there is a great deal of speculation about famous people now dead, who showed many traits of autism, perhaps the first person to publically acknowledge that she lives with the disorder is Dr. Temple Grandin. Dr. Grandin was featured in *Time* magazine's "100 Most Influential People in the World" in 2010

(Colorado State University 2011). A professor of animal science at Colorado State University, Dr. Grandin is known for two things: her foundational work in redesigning livestock handling plants and her efforts to educate the public about autism spectrum disorders. Grandin has spent considerable time and effort advocating for the humane slaughter of animals and for a better understanding of what autistic individuals have to offer the world; she uses her own life experiences as an example of how a family's efforts to advocate for, provide therapy for, and education for an autistic child can make a huge difference in the potential the child will be able to develop. In addition to her university web page, Dr. Grandin maintains a separate web presence for providing information on both her work with autism and animals (Grandin 2013).

Satoshi Tajiri, the creator of Pokémon, is on the high-functioning end of the spectrum (Moffat 2011). While Mr. Tajiri is reported to have confirmed that he is autistic, he prefers not to discuss this in any detail. He is in fact a fairly private person and not known for giving many interviews. In one of his rare interviews, an undated TIME Asia interview transcript posted on the Pokémon website, Mr. Tajiri said that when working he will work for 24 hours straight, then sleep for 12 hours (TIME Asia 2013). The TIME interviewer noted that for the interview Mr. Tajiri looked tired and had dark circles under his eyes.

The young jazz musician Matt Savage has been called an autistic savant; while at one time unable to bear the sound of music, he then showed a rare capacity for being able to play and create music on the piano (English 2012). It is interesting to note that Savage became more comfortable with music after his parents placed him in acoustic integration therapy. Early and consistent therapy can make a great difference in the outcome of young people on the spectrum.

Education also plays a therapeutic role, stretching a person's capacity and helping him or her discover previously untapped potential. Perhaps more so than with any other invisibly disabled group, students on the spectrum have outcomes that are nearly impossible to predict. A student may not be able to respond to all the demands of university; in leaving school the student may become the next Bill Gates. Most students, however, will end up falling somewhere in between these points on the spectrum.

CHAPTER FOUR

Attention Deficit/Hyperactive Disorder (AD/HD)

The diagnostic criteria for AD/HD are more complex, and longer, than for many other disorders. The criteria have multiple parts:

1. **There are nine criteria of which a child must meet six**—these include: forgets daily activities, does not seem to hear when spoken to, has trouble keeping attention even on play activities, makes regular careless mistakes, fails to follow instructions, struggles with organization, loses everyday items regularly (pencils, toys, etc.), avoids things which require focus, easily distracted (DSM-V Criteria for ADHD 2013).

2. **The child must meet these criteria for at least six months** *and* **the criteria have to be present to an extent that is exceptional given the child's age and developmental state.** If both of these conditions are met, then a child has met the attention deficit portion of the criteria.

There are a further nine criteria for being diagnosed as hyperactive and a child has to display six of the nine to be diagnosed as hyperactive. Three of these criteria are related to *impulsivity*, six to *hyperactivity*. Again, the child must display these symptoms for at least six months before diagnosis, and these criteria have to be present to an extent that is inappropriate for the child's developmental level (e.g. not "ordinary" fidgeting that is to be expected in a child of that age). The three criteria for impulsivity are: blurts out answers before a question is even finished; struggles to wait for turns; will interrupt the conversations/ games/activities of others uninvited. The six criteria for hyperactivity are: fidgets and squirms while others are able to be still; gets up and wanders in class; excessive energy/running; struggles to play quietly; talks a great deal; seems to always be moving.

There is even more to this diagnosis—some of these criteria need to have been present in the child before the child is seven years of age—in layman's terms, the child needs to have been noticeably distracted, restless, and unfocused compared to other young children from an early age. Also, in addition to all this, these behaviors need to be present *in at least two environments—not just in school*—the child needs to display these behaviors in another environment such as at home, at social functions, in worship settings, etc.

There is yet a further criterion—the behavior needs to be present to a level that is considered *impairing*. In other words, just because a child seems very distractible compared with same-age peers, if the child is still able to function in school and at home without impairment, then the child does not meet the criteria for AD/HD.

Finally, the child cannot be displaying these symptoms only in relation to a developmental or psychotic disorder, e.g. before a diagnosis of AD/HD is reached, a diagnostician has to take into account any mental illness, or developmental delays a child lives with as the possible source of inappropriate age-related behavior.

A child who is found to be AD/HD is thus so lacking in attention and focus and the ability to control their physical movement, that they have moved beyond being "fidgety" or "restless" and have reached the point of living with a disorder. A disorder by definition, disrupts the daily functioning of an individual, interfering with a person's capacity to carry out both mundane and challenging tasks.

Note that this diagnosis process also has to be carried out by a qualified professional. Parents should not allow a doctor who is in general practice to "diagnose" their child and place him/her on medication without formal testing by a qualified professional. Qualified professionals include neuro-psychologists, psychiatrists, and other medical doctors specifically trained to both give diagnostic testing and interpret the test results. Any doctor who asks a handful of questions, or gives a child or family one form to fill out and makes the diagnosis on the basis of such limited analysis has not followed correct diagnostic procedure and has not made a qualified diagnosis—at best they've made an educated guess.

It should also be noted, for diagnostic purposes, there are three types of AD/HD: *Combined Type* (both attention deficit and hyperactive/impulsive behavior is present); *Predominantly Inattentive Type*; *Predominantly Hyperactive–Impulsive Type* (Center for Disease Control and Prevention 2013). In other words, even with AD/HD there are multiple ways that the disorder can affect each individual. Knowing that a student is AD/HD only provides general information for families and educators—how each individual experiences the impacts of the disorder in their life, and in their studies, can only be learned by talking to the person; in the case of students, educators will find differences in learning styles among students who share this diagnosis.

Background

AD/HD as we currently diagnose it is fairly new. Interestingly, it is known that as early as 1798 Sir Alexander Crichton was already describing symptoms that we now associate with the disorder (Lange *et al.* 2010; History of ADHD 2009). Crichton observed a lack of the "necessary degree of constancy to any one object" that allowed a child to be successful in education. Crichton noted that when a person was born with this inability to focus, the person could usually still be educated; however, educating him would prove difficult (Crichton 1798). Crichton called this a "disease of inattention" such that everything from a door being opened to a person walking up and down in another room could distract the affected individual. Note that Crichton is recognizing what continues to be recognized—that this inability to focus is far beyond what is considered developmentally appropriate given an affected person's age. This provides evidence that it is a *social myth* that AD/HD is a recent development; at least since the end of the 18th century there have been children whose inability to focus or sit still was noticeably disabling to "normal" educational pursuits.

Lange's article 'The history of attention deficit hyperactivity disorder' does a good job of laying out the historical context of the co-development of a medical understanding of biologically based reasons for behavior and the realization that children, not just adults, could suffer from a range of observable disorders. In the early 19th century, Dr. Heinrich Hoffman "rejected the common opinion of his time that psychiatric patients were obsessed or criminal, but rather regarded mental disorders as medical issues" (Lange *et al.* 2010). Hoffman also wrote several children's stories and there remains debate if his story "Fidgety Phil" is a story of a naughty boy, or a boy showing all the symptoms of AD/HD—or perhaps both. There was a social presumption that a "morally good" child could learn to sit still. By

1908 doctors were recognizing that encephalitis could leave children with brain damage that affected their behavior and from then until the 1960s it was usually automatically assumed that children who showed the signs of what we now would classify AD/HD behavior were in some way brain damaged, even when doctors could not find "notable" evidence of this damage in anything but the child's hyperactivity.

By 1954, Ritalin was introduced and became the drug of choice for treating these hyperactive children—replacing the previously used drug Benzedrine; Ritalin continues to be given to hyperactive children, although there are now an increasing array of drugs for doctors to prescribe. Not all individuals respond well to Ritalin, and sometimes trial and error is necessary to find an appropriate medication for an individual.

By the 1960s, there was a change in the medical point of view that brain damage was necessarily part of a hyperactive child's make-up. The Oxford International Study Group of Child Neurology pushed for changing the dominant diagnostic criteria to reflect the understanding that a child could be hyperactive and not brain damaged—in 1963 the group argued that children without symptoms outside of hyperactive behavior should be diagnosed with "minimal brain dysfunction" rather than "brain damage"—indicating that while the affected child's brain might be different, the brain wasn't necessarily cognitively impaired. Doctors were recognizing that a child could be very intelligent *and* hyperactive. It was the 1970s before hyperactivity ceased to be the main focus of diagnosis, however, and more attention began to be paid to the difficulty with attention and focus these children were also living with. Yet, it wasn't until 1980 that the attention portion of the disorder was recognized by the medical community through the use of *diagnostic* terminology. The *Diagnostic and Statistical Manual of Mental Disorders* (DSM-III) of 1980 was the first to include attention deficit disorder.

By considering the history of changing medical views surrounding mental illness, what it means to be "brain damaged" and AD/HD diagnosis, it is easier to understand why there is the social impression that attention deficit disorder is a "new" disorder and that the number of children affected by the disorder is rapidly increasing. The diagnostic term is, relatively speaking, a newer term. With the relative newness of the diagnostic criteria it is logical that recognizing which children meet the criteria has been an educational matter within the medical community. As more doctors are educated to recognize the disorder and refer children for specialized testing, more children are being diagnosed. The characteristics of the condition, however, have been observed since the 18th century, and were doubtless present before this. AD/HD did not *diagnostically exist* before 1980, but the physical impact was still present in people's lives.

The relative newness of the diagnostic term is a separate issue from the growing concern that doctors who are not qualified make the diagnosis, or who even if qualified are not carrying out the proper testing before making the diagnoses. There is growing concern that even doctors who are qualified are none-the-less taking shortcuts and offering medication without going through the proper steps of diagnosis (Schwarz 2013). This has led to an ongoing contentious larger social argument that there is too much medication, given to too many children. Children who actually benefit from and require medication tend to get caught in the crossfire of this social debate about over-diagnosis and over-medication of children. Their personal identity becomes conflicted as they absorb the larger social argument that fewer children should be taking medication.

Group identity

The children who are diagnosed young are often dramatically reappraised in school environments after diagnosis—before diagnosis they are often labeled as having behavior problems and sometimes as intellectually impaired. Once diagnosed and given adequate medication, these children will often be seen in a new light at school, where grades typically improve and behavior becomes more in keeping with expectations. There remains a social stigma surrounding children with hyperactive behavior—they are considered ill-mannered, their parents are often considered ineffective in discipline/training, and there is often a perception that poor grades are reflective of lower intellect, rather than an inability to focus. As one professional stated, her own childhood diagnosis came as a "relief" to her, because it gave another reason besides "being stupid" for the struggles she was experiencing in school (Fearn 2013). She had internalized the perception that she was not a smart student, when in fact her disability was getting in the way of her ability to learn.

There is another side, however, to growing up "medicated" as some children currently do. As one blog and conversation exemplifies, young people can start to question the nature of their "authentic self" (Barnett 2012). As one young woman was left questioning—"Is the real me the unmotivated person who doesn't take meds, or the focused successful person who does?" To those outside the AD/HD community, it might seem clear that if a medicine makes productive functioning possible, then just take the medicine.

What people who do not take medication for an invisible disability do not realize is that those who are invisibly disabled have internalized the social myth that they look so much like others that they should be capable of acting like others, including functioning without daily medication. In effect, my "real" self is the one who *doesn't* take medicine because that is the way all the "normal people" get through life—without medication that impacts their reaction to their environment.

A study reported in the journal, *Advances in Nursing Science* also found that identity and medication were two themes that came up repeatedly amongst children diagnosed as AD/HD (Kendall *et al.* 2004). The health professionals who wrote the article state, "By far the most troubling aspects of these data were the meanings and the overidentification [sic] these children placed on having ADHD, as if they had an ADHD identity...These children often talked about ADHD in terms of who they were, rather than the symptoms they experienced" (Kendall *et al.* 2004, p.122). The children in the study also echoed what they heard from others, that they were "bad" and "fidgety"; although most children found medication helpful, many were ashamed of needing to take medicine. As one boy said, "I just want to be myself. My Mom makes me take it so I can focus" (Kendall *et al.* 2004, p.124). This is another example of how a child with AD/HD seems confused about the role medication has in shaping his identity—that he cannot be his *real* self on medication and cannot focus without medication.

To put this dilemma AD/HD children face in a different light, imagine that a child were diagnosed as living with type 1 diabetes and required insulin injections on a daily basis. Society would not judge that this was an example of a family who had failed to educate or train the child in correct eating methods; there would not be debate about whether diabetes was "real" or an excuse that parents were using it as a basis for medicating their child; families would not be socially judged to be using medication as a "quick fix" rather than just disciplining their child to eat a better diet. Children who use medication for what society has accepted as "real" medical conditions are not influenced by society to believe there is anything wrong in taking their medicine.

Children who live with invisible disabilities, particularly with AD/HD, continue to reflect the greater social stigma related to having an invisible disability (that can benefit from medication); using medication is seen by the person herself as either a crutch or a way of subduing her "true" nature and identity. Children who benefit from medication nonetheless believe the social myth that they should be able to function "normally" without medication.

Physiology

AD/HD is classified as a neuropsychological disorder; children with AD/HD are almost always found to also have "emotional or learning problems" (Voeller 2004, p.799). Studies, including studies of twins, find that AD/HD has a strong genetic basis, and that the inattentive qualities remain with an individual into adulthood (Voeller 2004, p.802). Studies have not clarified if adults outgrow hyperactivity or if some adults simply learn to control their hyperactive behavior to an acceptable level for social contexts.

MRI studies consistently can find small but measurable differences between the brains of children with AD/HD and control groups (Voeller 2004; Yu-Feng *et al.* 2007). SPECT imaging—which looks at blood flow in the brain—has also shown differences in how the brain of AD/HD children function both at rest and under stress (Amen and Carmichael 1997). These are examples of physical evidence that AD/HD is real—which has not yet vanquished the continuing social myth that this isn't a "real disability." Some members of the public (including some faculty and staff on college campuses) continue to say, "I don't believe in AD/HD" and then point to visible disabilities as the "real" disabilities. Whenever this ignorance about the nature of disability is encountered on a campus of higher education, it is the responsibility of administrators and management to establish educational opportunities for those who still fail to realize that AD/HD and other invisible disabilities are very real, very measurable, and just as important to acknowledge as are visible disabilities. The onus of providing this education cannot be left to the disability service provider alone to meet; resources and attitudes beyond this one office need to be brought to bear on creating a better educated campus. The tone of a campus also needs to be more inclusive before such educational efforts will take root.

Comorbid disorders

Studies find that it is most common for AD/HD to be present with other disorders. *The Journal of Child Psychology and Psychiatry* for example published the results of a Swedish study that followed a group of schoolchildren over a period of several years. Eighty-seven percent of the children who had AD/HD were found to be living with at least one comorbid disorder; 67 percent were living with two or more comorbid disorders (Kadesjo and Gillberg 2001, p.490). Two of the most common disorders present with AD/HD were "reading/writing (40%)" and "developmental coordination disorder (47%)" (Kadesjo and Gillberg 2001, p.490). As a disability service provider and educator, one of the things that stood out to me in this study was that of the 14 percent of children in this study who were found to be autistic, 7 percent were currently diagnosed as AD/HD and 7 percent were on the threshold for an AD/HD diagnosis; autism disorder was not present in the non-AD/HD group (Kadesjo and Gillberg 2001, p.490). As mentioned in Chapter Three, autism is seldom present without comorbid disorders—this study which was focused on AD/HD further supports this finding and suggests that autism and AD/HD are found together with noticeable frequency. The other notable factor, particularly from the point of view of education, was that 60 percent of the AD/HD children lived with *oppositional defiant disorder*, vs. 1 percent of the non-AD/HD group. This is defined as a "recurrent pattern of developmentally inappropriate levels of negativistic, defiant, disobedient, and hostile behavior toward authority figures" (Hamilton and Armando 2008, p.861).

Other studies have also found a high incident of comorbidity between oppositional defiant disorder (ODD) and AD/HD (Biederman 2005). Biederman, who has conducted research and compiled research results from others, also reports a 60 percent rate of comorbidity of ODD and AD/HD in children. Biederman reported that amongst adults with AD/HD there is a 55 percent rate of coexistence of anxiety disorders with AD/HD (Biederman 2005, p.1216). Children also show a high rate of comorbidity for anxiety, as well as learning disorders and mood disorders—all of which are also present in adults with AD/HD. Adults add alcohol and drug dependency to the mix, with adult males with AD/HD having addiction rates in approximately 35 percent of cases (Biederman 2005, p.1216).

For educators it is important to recognize that college age students are transitioning into independent adulthood; for some of them this transition will include becoming addicts who use drugs and/or alcohol to self-medicate in the face of the disorders they live with. If we consider that 35 percent of AD/HD males become addicts, and that an increasing proportion of our student body is living with AD/HD, these factors will increasingly make themselves known on our college campuses. Incident reports of breaches of conduct due to alcohol and drug use will likely increase for the foreseeable future. Health and wellness education on campus should also take into account that students with invisible disabilities are likely to have an added dimension of identity crises they are dealing with at this crucial developmental point in their lives.

Presentation

First, it is important to realize that due to the high coexistence of other disorders in the same students who live with AD/HD, it is sometimes difficult to tell which behavior is related to attention deficits, to anxiety, or to oppositional defiant disorder. The students I have met over the years seem to have a large comorbidity of anxiety with AD/HD. It may be that those who do not have an anxiety disorder before arriving at college are more likely to develop one once they are in the stressful environment where all students are experiencing new levels of anxiousness in the face of this major life transition.

AD/HD students and adults often present as disorganized in some areas of life—more likely to lose daily items like keys, phones, pens, notebooks—even though they can be sometimes very focused in events that capture their imagination and interest. It is helpful to realize that focus can come from several sources: medication, obsessive compulsive disorder, and autism spectrum disorder can all cause an otherwise scattered student/coworker to have areas/interests/times of intense concentration. In other words, one can be both inattentive to some items and obsessively compulsive about others. This can present a very interesting, and even aggravating attitude towards work and assignments. An individual cannot be counted on to be fascinated by work that needs to be done, or remember what might seem like essential details, even though they might be able to remember minutiae about topics that do capture their attention.

Individuals living with AD/HD are also more likely to be impulsive both in action and words; they are more likely to blurt out answers; speak without raising a hand or waiting to be recognized by a leader; jump into new tasks without necessarily following through and finishing up once a task becomes mundane. Focus over the long haul can be very problematic. Attention to detail can also be challenging. These same individuals are often able to see connections where others do not; to be able to come up with creative solutions to problems that others have not thought of; to bring creative energy and passion to those topics which engage them. Those with the disorder often bring a sense of vitality and a spark of intensity to projects, which can be helpful in keeping other team members invigorated.

Support

Those living with AD/HD often require external structure to offset the difficulty with focus that is commonplace with the disorder. When a context allows for only one way for things to be done, however, this will create handicapping circumstances for people living with the disorder. For example, having a list of duties or assignments that need to be completed during a clearly defined timeframe allows a person to have guidelines for what their agenda needs to be; trying to tell a person how to accomplish those goals creates strictures which will keep him or her from using their own creativity and energy to find their own best way to achieve the goal. As a teacher I have often found that students with AD/HD can find imaginative ways of problem solving when they have a clear goal to work towards and are allowed to find their own way to reach that goal.

Of course, like all individual members of a group, individual people within the larger group of those living with AD/HD may require more use of examples/samples to have a clear understanding of what is expected in a finished project. Remember, there are often comorbid disorder, including language processing disorders, anxiety, and obsessive compulsive disorder which may complicate a person's ability to either picture what someone else is describing or to recognize when they have reached the point of "good enough" for the purposes of some work or assignments. Examples and samples of completed work are very useful in helping to explain the expectations of specific contexts. A lack of clear guidelines for what meets expectations in a given context will dramatically increase the level of anxiety in most people; this is even more so when a person is living with AD/HD. As a population people within this group are very prone to anxiety and anxiety disorders. This tendency towards anxiety is amplified by previous life experiences; many people within this group have lived through being treated as less intelligent or less able than others due to the effect of the disorder on their ability to organize and concentrate. As mentioned earlier, people are more likely to identify with the disorder and see the inability to plan or focus as personal failings. These past experiences lead people to worry about being undervalued again, which increases the level of anxiety related to each new opportunity to be judged and found wanting they encounter.

In both the classroom and the work place, "low-risk" opportunities to practice as a person learns are important. While this concept of low-risk opportunity will be discussed further in Chapter Nine, at this point one example will be offered now. Having one's entire semester of learning judged on the basis of one exam—a final—is a very high-risk method of judgment for the student. They have only one opportunity to show they have learned a semester's worth of knowledge; they risk a great deal if they fail and as a result this high risk will be accompanied by high levels of stress, actually decreasing the likelihood of the student being able to accurately display what he knows. When a student is offered multiple practice assignments that are each worth a smaller portion of their overall grade, then these are lower risk assignments—the student risks a relatively low portion of her grade if she has misunderstood something and she is also freed from the higher level of anxiety related to high-risk assignments, increasing the probability that she will be able to give an accurate showing of what she has learned. Low-risk assignments increase opportunities for success over the course of the semester by decreasing anxiety.

Public figures

David Neeleman founded JetBlue, and like other successful entrepreneurs, athletes, and celebrities with AD/HD, he finds it easier to bring his creativity and energy to big projects than to focus on small details (Gilman 2005). He also feels being AD/HD allows him to see solutions that others do not and was supported by parents who encouraged him to value his own strengths, even as teachers would pressure him to conform more to standardized expectations.

Olympic gold medal swimmer Michael Phelps was diagnosed with AD/HD at the age of nine, after his mother took him to a doctor following a teacher's concern that Michael seemed incapable of focus (Dutton 2007). Mrs. Phelps, herself a teacher, did a great deal of advocating in the school system so that teachers would continue to work on helping Michael develop as a student; she also hired private tutors to support him educationally. Swimming was instrumental in helping Michael develop focus and giving him an outlet for his considerable energy.

Actor and comedian Howie Mandel decided to "go public" with his AD/HD diagnosis and also filmed information/education clips for the public about AD/HD in 2008 (Quily 2008). Mandel supports awareness of the disorder and points out that he was not diagnosed until he was an adult. He uses his celebrity to advocate that people do not allow the presence of the disorder in their life to stop them from having goals they work towards.

Energy, creativity, and new ideas are important strengths that accompany a disorder known for the challenges it creates related to focus and attention to details. Those living with AD/HD can harness this energy with support and invigorate work environments they are part of.

CHAPTER FIVE

Language Processing Disorders, Including Dyslexia

According to *The Praeger Handbook of Special Education* (2007):

> Language disorders are attributed to neurological disturbances that impact the efficient transmission of information to and from specific cortical regions in the brain… they impinge on decoding for reading, spoken and written text comprehension, classroom interactions, and problem-solving across subject areas. (Bursztyn 2007, p.64)

Language disorders include dyslexia and other reading and writing disabilities that affect a person's language processing. In every day usage, people tend to refer to all language disorders as "dyslexia." While dyslexia is one language disorder, technically, not all language disorders are dyslexia. Defining dyslexia, however, is problematic as there continue to be competing definitions (Ferrer *et al.* 2010; Lyon, Shaywitz and Shaywitz 2003; Tonnessen 1997). From an educational perspective, where we are interested in recognizing the impact of language processing disabilities on a student's classroom capacity/ challenges, one of the more useful proposed definitions of dyslexia was put forward in 2003 by Lyon *et al.*

> Dyslexia—is neurobiological in origin. It is characterized by difficulties with accurate and/or fluent word recognition and by poor spelling and decoding abilities. These difficulties typically result from a deficit in the phonological component of language that is often unexpected in relation to other cognitive abilities and the provision of effective classroom instruction. Secondary consequences may include problems in reading comprehension and reduced reading experience that can impede growth of vocabulary and background knowledge. (Lyon *et al.*, p.2)

This definition is useful for educators due to several points it makes: students who are dyslexic will display reading and writing skills that appear incongruous with their intelligence; these students tend *not* to learn best from written material and may rely heavily on classroom discussions/verbal explanations; these students may read material without gaining knowledge, or take much less from reading than their peers. Students who live with dyslexia/language processing disorders are also less likely to read for pleasure and more likely to have limited vocabularies and knowledge compared to same age peers who do read. Ferrer *et al.* in their "Uncoupling of reading and IQ over time" (2010) report that due to this decreased use of reading, students who are dyslexic will in effect limit the natural potential of their IQ compared to same-age peers, whose IQs appear to develop due to reading.

From here forward the term dyslexia will primarily be used to discuss language processing disorders. This term will be used for the same reason that the term is typically used—it is a shorter, easier way to refer to language processing disorders, and most individuals with a language processing disorder *self-identify* as dyslexic.

Background

German physician Oswald Berkhan first published case studies of pupils who had language processing disorders related to spelling in 1885–86; Berkhan called this difficulty "language stammer" (Warnke, Schutte-Korne and Ise 2012). Before Berkhan there were several differences in how language disorders were studied and what they were labeled. Previously referred to as "word blindness" to indicate that a person could see a word and not recognize it, this type of disorder had been studied in adults. The adults developed word blindness as a result of head injury or illness and had previously been able to read language without difficulty (Anderson and Meier-Hedde 2001, pp.9–10). Berkhan was not only publishing the first case studies of children, but his studies were of children who had no notable head injury or illness, and who otherwise seemed to be of reasonable intellect. Berkhan would also go on to found his own institute for "ill and handicapped" persons in Erkerode, Germany, and one can speculate that Berkhan was ahead of his time in recognizing learning disabilities (Berkhan [1887] 2011).

It was Rudolf Berlin, in an 1887 publication, who proposed the term "dyslexia" in place of the previously used phrase "word blindness"; it was from this point forward that dyslexia would become a term used to describe a range of disabilities related to reading (Wagner 1973). At the same time, there was a gradual movement to define and recognize the specific disability dyslexia as it pertained to a developmental disorder present in children vs. a disorder that was acquired later in life due to illness or injury. Current literature tends to further this distinction by referring to "developmental dyslexia" when referring to the type of dyslexia which is naturally present rather than that which developed later in life as a result of illness or injury (Lyon *et al.* 2003).

Group identity

Children who are born with dyslexia may go a number of years without being diagnosed; both before and after diagnosis many endure difficulties and negative associations related to the educational process. A negative self-identity and adverse associations with education were commonly reported in studies of identity conducted amongst both teens and adults who are dyslexic (Nalavany *et al.* 2011; Ingesson 2007). These are not the only documented studies that show, "young people with dyslexia manifest lower self-esteem than others" (Ingesson 2007, p.575.) Ingesson's study of Swedish young adults with dyslexia found 40 percent not only had negative self-images due to their struggles with academics, but that they were pessimistic about their futures due to these struggles.

At the same time, Ingesson's study showed that as children learn more about how to manage reading and writing, and as a result had better school performance, their self-image improved and they became more optimistic about the future. Dyslexia continued, however, to have a significant impact on their choices and identity, with 80 percent of the study-subjects reporting that dyslexia had quite a bit of influence over what they chose to study after primary school (Ingesson 2007, p.581). All the subjects of the study continued to be challenged by spelling and slow reading, even if their school performance did improve.

Once adults, those who live with dyslexia continue to struggle with how the disability impacts their identity. As Nalavany reports, "Research has shown that approximately 50 percent of adults disclose their dyslexia to colleagues or supervisors" which means that half of affected adults choose to keep the disability private in a work setting (Nalavany *et al.* 2011, p.75). This indicates that even with increasing protection from discrimination under the law, employees are reluctant to inform employers of their language processing disability. As Nalavany interpreted this, "Dyslexia has become a risk factor to success and a well-lived life" (Nalavany *et al.* 2011, p.75). Nalavany also reminds us that, "Because dyslexia does not resolve with time, the need for supportive services across the lifespan is paramount" (Nalavany *et al.* 2011, p.76). Ironically, while adult employees might benefit from support, concern about repercussions in the workplace keep half of employees from disclosing their disability.

As a professional with three graduate degrees, the choice to disclose that I live with dyslexia was still not an easy one to make. Living with a disability continues to have a social stigma, and there remains concern in work environments that those who are disabled will not be able to "pull their weight." Yet, it is because of this stigma that I also realized that I needed to speak out and publically declare that I was disabled. If those of us who do make our way to professional positions remain silent, we reinforce the stereotype that professional careers, including academics, are not a reasonable goal for those who are dyslexic or disabled.

Being dyslexic created a greater burden on both myself and the chair of my dissertation committee when I worked on my doctorate degree. There were times when I did not seem to be able to "see" the expectations of the dissertation format the way other graduate students did. I also required more rewrites of each chapter than appeared average. I would also point out, though, that I saw areas of research and had ideas that were truly unique to my field. As a result I was able to do what research is ideally meant to do—contribute new knowledge to my area of study. Now, I'm in a position to do something I find even more significant; I regularly mentor young people who live with disabilities, including dyslexia, and remind them that while hard work is necessary, professional success, including potentially a career in academics, is an achievable goal.

Physiology

Studies have found there are differences in both the brain and the way the brain processes language between those who are dyslexic and those who are not (Brown *et al.* 2001a; Temple *et al.* 2003). Those with a language processing disorder do not process language in the same area of the brain as those without a language processing disorder. A reoccurring observation made during brain imaging is finding that those with language processing disorders appear to process language "in frontal and/or right hemisphere regions to compensate for the dysfunctional left posterior reading systems" (Richlan 2009, p.3300).

Richlan *et al.*'s study reports that "overactivation in the primary motor cortex and the anterior insula" were observed as were "underactivation in the inferior frontal gyrus" (Richlan 2009, p.3307.) For the purposes of our discussion regarding educational outcomes for those living with a language processing disorder, it is less important exactly which region of the brain is underactive and more noteworthy that scientists can now see that the brain can function in different ways when trying to accomplish the same kinds of work. This also helps us understand why language processing takes longer in a dyslexic brain—the brain is not working with the area that is optimally designed to process language and therefore the activity of processing language is more "labor intensive" for the brain. In other words, it appears that a larger area that is less specialized in the task of working with language is trying to do the work that the language processing center is not doing.

Comorbid disorders

As mentioned in Chapter Four, AD/HD and dyslexia are measurably comorbid. At least one study is suggesting that even more commonly, auditory processing disorder (APD) is present in half those who also live with dyslexia (King *et al.* 2003). King *et al.*'s study of APD suggests that this is another disorder that is related to the brain having difficulty with processing stimuli in the region of the brain normally responsible for that type of stimulus; children respond best to speech and language therapy which may be teaching the brain to reroute the information to other regions of the brain (Moore 2006). As with dyslexia, there is increasing reason to believe that the center of the brain designed to process sound is not functioning as it should and that other areas of the brain, not designed to process sound, can none-the-less adapt to carry out the process, albeit more slowly and less effectively.

Ramus argues that one of the reasons there is room to disagree about what defines dyslexia is because separate disorders co-occur so regularly that what are in fact comorbid disorders are being interpreted as an extension of dyslexia (Ramus 2004). Challenges with physical stability, processing auditory information, and fine motor coordination so frequently appear problematic for dyslexic children, that there is disagreement as to whether these symptoms are part of dyslexia or frequent co-occurrence of other disorders (Ramus, Pidgeon and Frith 2003; Ramus *et al.* 2003). This ongoing disagreement continues to lead to differing definitions of dyslexia and questions as to whether dyslexia is strictly a language processing disorder or if it includes other symptoms, including what is currently diagnosed as a separate disorder, SLI (specific language impairment). Ramus has interpreted his study results to indicate that SLI and dyspraxia are separate, frequently co-occurring disorders and not part of dyslexia.

Many children with dyslexia, however, are also diagnosed with dyspraxia—"difficulty with the acquisition of patterns of movement" (Politt, Pollock and Waller 2004, p.38). Children with dyspraxia respond best to physical or occupational therapy, just as dyslexic children with an auditory processing disorder respond best to speech therapy in learning to better process audio stimuli. Once again, the brain seems to be capable of creating new pathways that allow for processing motor-sensory stimuli in a region or process that while not optimal, is still functional. Children with dyspraxia who receive appropriate therapy are thus able to develop improved physical coordination; practice with words similarly allows children with dyslexia to develop improved language processing.

Presentation

Considering the frequent comorbidity of challenges with balance, coordination, listening to and interpreting verbal communication (as well as a high rate of attention deficit disorder), it perhaps becomes clearer why in earlier education particularly, it is often assumed that a dyslexic child is not doing well in class because he or she simply isn't paying attention or "listening" to instructions. Difficulty with handwriting due to problems with processing written symbols is compounded by coordination difficulties—children who have trouble sitting still and have "sloppy handwriting" are usually accused of simply not putting in sufficient effort to their writing attempts, or not bothering to focus on what they are doing. Particularly since these children are otherwise intelligent, teachers may be left with the impression they are dealing with a fidgety or lazy child, rather than a disabled child. This view of the child's lack of effort, or lack of focus, can color expectations for the child's work, another reason why it may take several years for schoolwork to make apparent that there is a disability contributing to the child's behavior and what they produce for schoolwork.

While it is often clearer by college age that a young person is dyslexic, it is not necessarily recognized that the student may struggle with processing what they are told, and thus an appearance of "not listening in class," can affect a professor's impression of a dyslexic student. Speech and physical therapy may have had some positive impact on an individual's abilities; however, some young people continue to struggle with understanding audio stimuli and with coordination, while others have never had an opportunity for therapy. Handwriting continues to be problematic for most dyslexic people; as a result students living with dyslexia usually prefer to use a word processing program rather than handwriting to complete any written assignments. In-class writings can be very challenging for dyslexic students. Some are not physically capable of producing what would be considered legible handwriting, or require so much effort, time and focus to produce legible handwriting that doing so is physically and mentally exhausting. It is common for dyslexic students to require extended time to process both verbal and written information.

It may be the high incidence of specific language impairment and auditory processing disorder that lead to even non-AD/HD dyslexic students being more prone to distractibility. Consider how exhausting it becomes to focus on every bit of communication when all communication requires focus to be understood. It is natural that the brain will at times "take a break" from processing the constant deluge of sensory stimuli that floods in during the average day in college.

Support

When faculty and staff understand that it is likely that a dyslexic person has to work harder to process *all* forms of communication, it becomes more readily evident that someone living with dyslexia will benefit from support which indicates what are the "most important" bits of data that they should be working to hold on to, out of all the information they are presented with. There is a reason that many dyslexic persons prefer short, bulleted lists of key points.

- Specific information is often communicated more clearly.

- Additional white space around the sentence aids in deciphering words.

- Writers work harder to pull out the main points, reducing the work for the reader.

It is not reasonable to expect any student to listen to a 50 minute lecture and retain the majority of what is said; the person who is able to do so is uncommon. For someone with dyslexia it is almost always physically impossible to retain long strings of spoken words. Reinforcing key words and concepts are extremely helpful practices.

In the classroom speaking of an idea, presenting it on a board/ slide at the front of the class, and making it available in writing for reference after a class (through a handout or online) allows a student with dyslexia to reinforce their processing of the information. Remember, living with dyslexia often means that none of the ways of processing information that the person relies on works optimally and therefore having multiple ways to process information might be necessary in order for the person to fully grasp the information that is being relayed to them. It is also important, particularly for those of us who teach, to remember that dyslexic students who arrive in college are not intellectually impaired, even though their reading and writing skills might at first create this impression. It can be very frustrating for those with dyslexia when they are struggling to express a complex thought or idea. Spoken and written language require effort to be processed and when a person is tired, stressed, or under great pressure, these processes may slow down. The ideas are still there, they just require more time and effort to be communicated.

When one lives inside a dyslexic brain, it is very complicated to try and explain to those with non-dyslexic brains how inner idea processing works. Inside my mind, the thoughts I think do not require me to use language to think them. Dr. Temple Grandin (2013), while describing her autism, has done perhaps the best job of communicating a way of thinking that is shared with many dyslexic brains—thinking in pictures. I cannot confirm that this is how all dyslexic brains process information; however, everyone I have spoken to who lives with a language processing disorder describes something similar to picture thinking, versus thinking in words.

From conversations with others who are not dyslexic, I understand that many people think primarily in language. It is probably just as difficult to imagine how someone can meaningfully think complex ideas in pictures primarily as it is for me to imagine how anyone can think complex ideas when restricted to primarily language thoughts. I'm sure each way of processing ideas has advantages and disadvantages. With words having such limited capacity for carrying meaning, however, it always seems to me that word-thinking has to have peculiar limitations. In other words, the way of processing ideas that a person is accustomed to will strike him or her as "most natural."

Picture thinking or word thinking work; what works best for an individual is what they are accustomed to—there are also other methods of processing ideas, that serve many people well. For example some people associate sensory stimuli with color or sound (Svartdal and Iversen 1989). The methods of transferring knowledge in university from professor to student, however, seem to have been designed by those who think primarily in language; it does not appear to have occurred to them that not all people could learn by sitting and listening to spoken words. Pictures of lecture hall based classes dating back hundreds of years show that the model of a teacher standing at a lectern and speaking to a room of seated students has been the predominate way of transferring knowledge for many generations. Despite being a long-established tradition, this does not make the lecture hall based class the most effective learning method for the average student; it certainly does not serve dyslexic students well. Chapter Eight will discuss in more detail how professors can universally design even lecture hall based classes to benefit more students' learning.

Public figures

From the *Yale Center for Dyslexia and Creativity*:

> Dr. Carol Greider is one of the three winners of the 2009 Nobel Prize in Physiology or Medicine, joining just nine other women in winning the prize since its inception in 1901. Greider has never seen her gender as an obstacle; but in her early years of schooling, as well as in graduate school admissions, there was one obstacle to overcome: her dyslexia. (Crockett 2008)

Greider is one of many people living with dyslexia whose GRE[1] scores did not accurately reflect her capacity or knowledge. Of the 25 graduate

---

1   Graduate Record Examination—a standardized, national test proctored by the testing agency which designed it, the GRE score is used by many North American universities to decide whether or not they will consider individual students. Many schools set standard cut-off scores and do not consider students who have not achieved this score, regardless of any other information available about the student. (Dyslexic students typically struggle with the GRE.)

schools she applied to as a student, only two would consider her—Cal Tech and U.C. Berkeley—but she did have excellent grades, even if her GRE scores were low. Greider in fact started the work that would earn her the Nobel Prize as a graduate student at Berkeley. Dr. Greider now runs her own research laboratory at Johns Hopkins University School of Medicine where she is Director of Molecular Biology and Genetics (Greider 2013).

Richard Branson, head of the Virgin Empire, described in an interview with TED's Chris Anderson that due to his dyslexia he had a "miserable" time at school and left at age 15 (TED 2007). Branson also says that despite "running the largest group of private companies in Europe" he could not remember the difference between "net and gross" until someone took him aside after a meeting and drew pictures explaining that net was like a net in the sea pulling in fish—what was left in the net was his profit. With that visual image Branson finally remembered the difference. In 2007 when he gave the TED interview Branson estimated Virgin's gross worth to be 25 billion dollars. Branson is also an example that not every dyslexic person struggles with physical dexterity. Aside from his adult sporting pursuits, before leaving school he was the captain of the cricket and football teams (TED 2007).

Writer and movie director Steven Spielberg says, in an interview posted online, that finally being diagnosed with dyslexia as an adult caused the "puzzle pieces to fall into place." He knew in childhood that something was "wrong" but he went to primary school in the 1950s before developmental dyslexia was even recognized as a disorder. While he encountered a great deal of teasing due to his inability to read in front of the class, he reports also developing a large social group; it was this group he refers to as the "goon squad" that was the basis of his 1985 movie *The Goonies* (Friends of Quinn 2012). Spielberg said that many of these same friends grew up to discover that they too were living with disabilities and that "several" of them are also dyslexic. Making movies was Spielberg's way of creating his own space and being recognized for what he could do versus being singled out for where he struggled.

Living with dyslexia does not prevent creativity, great intelligence, and or even, for some, athletic prowess. Dyslexic students may at first appear to simply not be paying attention. Scratching beneath the surface of this appearance, though, will reveal a young person who is struggling to communicate with the world.

CHAPTER SIX

Generalized Anxiety Disorder and Obsessive Compulsive Disorder

According to the *Diagnostic and Statistical Manual of Mental Disorders-V* the family of *anxiety disorders* includes: generalized anxiety disorder, anxiety disorder not otherwise specified, social anxiety disorder, panic disorder, agoraphobia; separate and sometimes comorbid disorders include obsessive compulsive disorder (OCD), hoarding disorder, trichotillomania (hair-pulling), and excoriation (skin-picking) (American Psychiatric Association 2013).

For the purposes of a college environment, the most likely anxieties to be present in significant numbers amongst students *on campus* are generalized anxiety disorder and obsessive compulsive disorder. The reality is that when a person's anxiety is too significant, including agoraphobia which keeps a person from leaving their home, or social anxiety disorder which makes it very challenging to be in public or groups, a person isn't likely to find him or herself on campus. As veterans of military service return to school we are likely to see an increase in post-traumatic stress disorder; the impact of PTSD on individual campuses appears to be limited to date. It can be speculated that this is due in part to the veteran students' reluctance to seek out any form of counseling or assistance through campus resources. Some veterans also remain connected with the military through their registration as reservists (Zulyen-Wood 2011). Those still active with the military worry that there could be negative consequences if others find out they are living with PTSD (Zulyen-Wood 2011). Many campuses are doubtless ignorant regarding the degree of difficulty the wounded warriors on their campus face, including the challenges that PTSD creates regarding the affected students' ability to be on campus, or participate in classes.

Other students also arrive on campus living with PTSD—this is not an anxiety disorder that is limited to soldiers—again, the number of students affected is difficult to measure as many students are reluctant to bring up traumatic incidents from their past. Thus, students living with PTSD are more likely to present themselves as living with an "anxiety disorder" rather than PTSD if they do identify their disabled status to faculty or staff.

The current *DSM-V* diagnostic criteria for *generalized anxiety disorder (GAD)* are:

- Excessive anxiety for more days than not for at least six months.

- The individual affected finds it difficult to control worry.

- Anxiety and worry are associated with three or more of the following six symptoms:

  ○ restlessness/being keyed up/edgy

  ○ easily fatigued

  ○ trouble concentrating/mind goes blank

  ○ irritable

  ○ muscle tension

  ○ sleep disturbance.

In addition to the above listed symptoms, the diagnosing clinician must rule out substance abuse and other mental illnesses as the source of anxiety. The anxiety must also reach "clinically significant" levels of distress (Montgomery 2009, p.2)

As mentioned in Chapter Two, there is significant difference between "normal" anxiety, or nervousness—which we all experience—and an anxiety disorder, which only some of us will develop. According to Montgomery in the *Handbook of Generalized Anxiety Disorder*, studies in Europe and North America show 4–6 percent of people will eventually experience an episode of GAD (Montgomery 2009, p.5). The Cleveland Clinic Center for Continuing Education provides a clear explanation of the difference between normal anxiety and when anxiety becomes a disorder:

Anxiety is a natural response and a necessary warning adaptation in humans. Anxiety can become a pathologic disorder when it is excessive and uncontrollable, requires no specific external stimulus, and manifests with a wide range of physical and affective symptoms as well as changes in behavior and cognition (Rowney *et al.* 2010).

The NIMH estimates that approximately 18 percent of Americans—or 40 million people— live with an anxiety disorder (NIMH 2013a). The National Health Service (NHS) reports that GAD affects approximately "one in 20 adults in Britain," while one in ten will experience a panic attack (NHS 2013a, b). Note that at this point we are simply establishing that anxiety disorders, by whatever name, affect a notable segment of the population and that eventually one who works at the university level will encounter both students and coworkers who are living with some form of anxiety disorder.

Obsessive compulsive and other disorders are also showing up increasingly often amongst college students, faculty, and staff. The NHS sets out the four step pattern that *obsessive compulsive disorder* usually follows; this explanation clarifies the difference between a normal level of concern and when a thought pattern has reached the obsessive level of a disorder:

- Obsession—where your mind is overwhelmed by a constant obsessive fear or concern, such as the fear your house will be burgled.

- Anxiety—the obsession provokes a feeling of intense anxiety and distress.

- Compulsion—you then adopt a pattern of compulsive behavior to reduce your anxiety and distress, such as checking all the windows and doors are locked at least three times before you leave your house.

- Temporary relief—the compulsive behavior brings temporary relief from anxiety, but the obsession and anxiety soon return, causing the pattern or cycle to begin again (NHS 2012a).

Montgomery's *Handbook* relates that studies estimate approximately 2.7 million people in the European Union live with OCD (Montgomery 2009, p.5), while the NIMH estimates that approximately 2.2 million Americans live with the disorder (NIMH 2012b). People can develop a range of obsessive behaviors from hand washing to needing to follow an exact pattern when walking from one spot on campus to another. As the NHS explanation points out, the obsessive behavior grows out of an emotional need to relieve anxiety. As a person's stress level increases, the frequency and duration of obsessive behavior will increase; when very distressed, a person living with OCD can become physically incapacitated, unable to move beyond the repetitive behavior, because the behavior is no longer able to provide adequate relief given the degree of anxiety they are feeling.

There are students for example who will become obsessed with trying to perfectly fill in with pencil the small circles on a standardized test answer sheet (a Scantron sheet). This in turn can quickly degenerate into a repetitive cycle—the more the student becomes distressed about the fact they are spending too much time trying to perfectly fill in the answer sheet, the slower and more excruciated they become as they are compulsively obligated to try and fill in the answer sheet. Some students will begin erasing answers, refilling, then re-erasing until they've put holes in their answer sheet. Others will be unable to move past the first few questions. When a student is spending too much time and energy trying to fill in the small circles perfectly, the quickest solution is to allow the student to circle their answers directly on the test, and forego using the answer sheet altogether. The longer term solution is assisting the student in obtaining counseling so that he or she may work on managing the anxiety with which they are living.

Background

Rowa and Antony provide a good encapsulation of the modern history of generalized anxiety disorder (GAD) (Rowa and Antony 2008). When first introduced into the 1980 DSM-III, GAD was a catch-all diagnosis for anxiety which did not fit into another category; in the 1994 DSM-IV GAD is no longer a "residual category" but has criteria of "chronic and excessive worry" (Rowa and Antony 2008, p.78). The updated DSM-IV TR further defined GAD, including specifying the minimum length of duration of episodes as six months. There were only slight wording changes between DSM-IV and DSM-V related to GAD, changes which are unlikely to impact dignosis.

Explanation

Current Insights in Obsessive Compulsive Disorder begins with a review of the history of OCD diagnosis and reminds us that there are many historical accounts of behavior that we would now diagnose as OCD (Pittman 1994). In other words, although like all anxiety disorders the DSM criteria are relatively new, the behaviors associated with the disorder appear to have been present and recorded since at least the 15th century (Pittman 1994, p.3). In 1878 Carl Westphal "argued for an independent existence of the condition outside affective disorder," while also noting the overlap of what we now call Tourette's syndrome in people who also lived with other obsessive compulsive symptoms (Pittman 1994, p.6). It was Georges Gilles de La Tourette in 1885 who described the particular vocal and physical tics that would eventually be recognized as a separate neurological syndrome from OCD (Pittman 1994, p.6). There would prove to be however, significant comorbidity between Tourette's syndrome and OCD.

Group identity

To parallel the release of the fifth edition of the *Diagnostic and Statistical Manual of Mental Disorders (DSM-V)*, the search engine and news-site Yahoo published a series of first-person accounts of how individuals experienced living with mental illness. One woman shared how anxiety disorder had kept her from going to a movie theater for the past decade, and resulted in panic attacks when driving—both as driver and passenger (Darien 2013). She expressed her frustration that some religious leaders seemed to portray mental illness, including anxiety, as resulting from a lack of faith in God. As a faith-based person she turned to spiritual poetry for comfort and tried to support others by arranging with friends for public spiritual poetry reading; she had to rely on friends to host the events due to her anxiety disorder. She also reported having mixed results with medication, including suffering side effects that were so strong that she has at times stopped taking the medication, relying on faith to deal with her disorder.

Those with anxiety also make use of strategy sheets, breathing exercises, yoga, meditation, writing, social support networks, deep muscle relaxation, and personal behavior modification to assist in coping with the most debilitating aspects of the disorder (Tull 2009). There are a number of books and programs available, with a range of approaches to assist people with trying to manage the disorder. Approaches include cognitive, meditative, and physical activity. Again, it is more often social myth than reality that people with anxiety disorder simply have not learned to relax, or do not make adequate attempts to control their personal level of anxiety.

Viewing online sites that share personal accounts including *YouTube* and *Tumblr* is again informative of how frustrating those living with anxiety disorder find the social perception that they simply are not good at managing their personal anxiety. There is also repeated expression of frustrations over the social tendency to remark that ordinary events cause someone to "have a meltdown" or "have a panic attack". Those living with anxiety disorder express concern that it is this casual reference to a serious disorder which further blurs the social distinction between anxiety disorder and normal levels of anxiety all people experience. One of the debilitating aspects of anxiety disorder is that it requires so much time and effort on the part of an affected individual to manage what for other people are ordinary events—like driving in a car. Consider how challenging it is to attend school as an adult when even getting to school is an ordeal.

Physiology

A British study published in 1997 found differences in blood flow in the brain, indicating different regions of the brain reacting in times of stress among those with PTSD and OCD compared with healthy controls (Lucey *et al.* 1997). Similarly, a summary of studies found that it is a consistent finding that there is impairment in how the orbitofronto-striatal region of the brain functions in those with OCD compared to healthy controls (Mezies *et al.* 2008). More research has been called for in this area by researchers as they try to more closely identify exactly what is happening in the brain during anxiety in those who live with disorders; it is clear that the brain of those who live with anxiety disorders are responding to stimuli differently than do the brains of healthy controls. One study of young people with GAD suggests that the "structure and function" of the amygdala may also be linked to anxiety disorder (De Bellis *et al.* 2000). This same study reports that adults with GAD showed activity in the amygdala region when shown "neutral" faces—activity which was not present in healthy control subjects (De Bellis *et al.* 2000, p.56). The brain of those living with anxiety disorders appear to react to non-threatening situations and stimuli with a response usually reserved for threatening situations. Those with anxiety can be expected to "overreact" compared to others, because their brain is actually responding as if the body is under threat from what others perceive as an ordinary set of stimuli/events. When our perceptions vary regarding which events are stressful, concerning, or dangerous, then our reactions will also vary.

Comorbid disorders

One can find the term "comorbidity is the rule" in reference to both anxiety and depression (Alna and Susman 2006), and anxiety and AD/HD (Kaplan 2012). Additionally, affective disorders such as bipolar disorder and schizophrenia have a high rate of co-occurrence with anxiety disorders (Brown *et al.* 2001a).

A 2004 study of those living with eating disorders found not only a high rate of anxiety disorders comorbid in the population, but a compelling number of those with eating disorders said they developed an anxiety disorder in their youth, *before* they developed an eating disorder (Kaye *et al.* 2004). Some of the most notable statistics to come out of the study were that amongst those with eating disorders the "64 percent rate of lifetime anxiety disorders... [and] 41 percent frequency of OCD in people with eating disorders is much higher than the frequency found in community samples" (Kaye *et al.* 2004, p.2219). The higher rates of anxiety disorders and early onset of anxiety disorders amongst those who go on to develop eating disorders led the study authors to observe that anxiety disorders are possibly "a vulnerability factor for developing anorexia nervosa or bulimia nervosa" (Kaye *et al.* 2004, p.2215). This is noteworthy for college educators and administrators for several reasons: the age of onset of an eating disorder will often overlap with the age when students being attending college; stress has long been known to increase difficulty managing an eating disorder. These facts remind us that in order to assist students with eating disorders we must provide access to treatment for the underlying stress that may well be a foundational element of their eating disorder. Eating disorders are at the very least, closely related to anxiety disorders and one disorder cannot be treated without acknowledging the presence and complications of the other.

Presentation

Anxious people are sometimes only too obvious. For those who can read the body language of others it is not only possible to see anxiety but to "feel" it in another person. Anxiety can present as nervousness, restlessness, and even depression. People may voice concerns and want to talk through a possible scenario multiple times as a way of trying to relive their anxiety. For example, a person might ask, "What do I do if..." and seek specific recommendations and a course of action to follow in a given context. While we might expect this behavior in younger children who have limited life experience, we also tend to expect adults to outgrow their need to voice their concerns in this way. Yet, adults with anxiety often benefit from being allowed to talk through "What if" scenarios too.

OCD can present in a range of ways and varies considerably in presentation from person to person. Interestingly, at least several television shows have incorporated OCD as a character trait of police who work as detectives; their obsessive characteristics will sometimes explode in response to the stress of their environment. The American television show Monk and the BBC show Whitechapel, for example, both featured lead detectives who live with, and have their work complicated by, obsessive compulsive disorder. While the characters have many disimilarities, their desire for order and their ability to focus on detail are both reasonably common traits to be found amongst those living with the disorder.

It is also common, however, to find that those living with OCD might have large stacks of books, magazines, newspapers, and files surrounding them in what to an outsider may appear a chaotic fashion. To the person whose items these are, however, there is often an order and logic to their arrangement of items which allows them to find a specific item when they seek it; as a result when another person tries to "organize" this seeming chaos, it creates considerable distress for the person, who feels they have then "lost" everything in the new organizational system. Again, students, professors, and staff can all exhibit both extremes of OCD – from the orderly where nothing can be moved without distressing the owner of the items, to the apparent chaos that does not prevent the owner from quickly putting their hand on one item out of the many.

When a person becomes very distressed over having their items moved, or their routine upset, it is always possible that this is an outward sign of the inner struggle they are having with OCD or anxiety. Having physical things and appointments arranged a specific way—no matter how disarrayed it may appear to others – is another way of controlling internal stress. Just as an obsessive behavior such as multiple hand washing, or walking a specific route across campus can temporarily relieve stress, providing a particular external order to events and items can also provide release or a sense of control over anxiety. Consider when negotiating with someone who seems unable to alter the order of events or placement or presence of items that they may in fact be (consciously or not) trying to control their anxiety. Anxiety also is increasingly recognized as an underlying element of the disorder that leads to a person hoarding.

Arguing with someone about how illogical their obsession, anxiety, or clinging to items is does not address the underlying disorder and is not likely to lead to any long-term change in a person's behavior. When behavior reaches the point of being a disorder, it is necessary for a mental health professional to become involved in working with the person so that he or she is able to regain management of their behavior, rather than being controlled by their compulsion.

Support

Recently I met again with a young man who lives with comorbid anxiety and a language processing disorder. He has worked very hard to ensure he will have an opportunity to continue his studies into graduate school. He stopped in, as he does on occasion throughout the semester, to voice his anxiety about not getting into graduate school. "What if I fail a class this semester?" I reminded him he could repeat a class to improve his grade. "What if…" He voiced a dozen concerns, from not finding a graduate school that would accept him (I reminded him of the probability of acceptance he already had in two programs), to not finding funding (again, he had two probable offers). As we talked through his concerns, he slowly started to calm himself. I reminded him that he needed to continue to keep his appointments in counseling services so that he would continue to work on techniques that would help him manage his anxiety in the future. We also discussed that perhaps he would eventually need medication to help him manage his anxiety. At this time, he feels that being able to talk through his concerns is allowing him to manage his anxiety without medication. While he is the student who needs to 'check in' with me most often, he is not the only student who lives with anxiety disorder who needs to stop in and just talk routine matters through on occasion in this 'What if' litany of concerns. Having a person who can calmly respond as a sounding board is very helpful in assisting someone with anxiety disorder in coping – particularly when it is only one of multiple techniques the person is using to manage their disorder.

Students may or may not have documentation which would make them eligible for disability support services; since we cannot directly ask students if they have a disability, we have to ensure that our syllabi have statements regarding the availability of disability support services on campus.

Students with anxiety disorders are also more likely to need non-distracting test environments and extended test time. Anxiety levels can skyrocket as they note other students finishing a test before them, as ambient environmental noises become distracting, and as they become hypersensitive to noise and movement around them under the stress of being tested. It is also possible for students with anxiety to have a comorbid level of attention deficit disorder and thus be prone to added distraction in a normal test environment. Allowing students to test in cubicles and wear noise-reducing headphones can be useful strategies in order to acquire a better sense of what the student is actually learning; too often, testing an anxious student in a normal test environment actually is testing their anxiety level rather than their knowledge.

The higher-risk an assignment – in a work or testing environment – the more naturally stress-producing it is. In a classroom context, this means that classes where a semester's grade is based on only a couple of items, perhaps a midterm and final exam, means that those few assignments are very high-value (worth a large part of the grade) and thus very stressful. Planning a class so that students have a number of lower-value opportunities to show their knowledge can help keep stress levels more manageable for all students, and is particularly beneficial for students who can be moved to panic attacks over high-value assignments. Knowledge is not necessarily adequately reflected if grading and testing are largely increasing stress via avoidable factors such as just several high-value assignments, by only being able to show that knowledge has been acquired using one format – a standardized test – and by denying people an opportunity to show smaller acquisitions of knowledge.

These same truths hold in a work environment. Employers/supervisors can encourage employee retention and increase the rate at which employees learn and adapt to new knowledge/skills by creating opportunities to learn as the employees work. Hands-on learning, practice as a person learns, and allowing the learning of new work by working alongside someone more experienced, all reduce the stress of acquiring new knowledge and increase the likelihood that the new knowledge will stay with the learner.

Public figures

In 2006 football (soccer) player David Beckham made it public knowledge that he lives with obsessive compulsive disorder (Firth 2006). Beckham described some of the ways the disorder affects his daily life including needing to have the soft drinks in his fridge at a specific number—no more, no less—having things in pairs, lined up neatly, or completely out of sight so that any hint of disorder is not distracting him. Beckham also spends time arranging leaflets and books in hotel rooms, needing to order the environment around himself in order to reduce his own anxiety. Beckham also said that while his team-mates at Real Madrid had not been aware of his disorder, his former team-mates at Manchester United used to intentionally rearrange his items in order to deliberately provoke him.

It may be hard to discern how someone who has lived with anxiety since early childhood could choose to go on to have a career in acting, however, Oscar-winner Kim Basinger did just that. Speaking of how she has struggled with the disorder since childhood, Basinger's motto is to work through her fear (Fisher 2012). As a schoolgirl Basinger remembers that just being asked to speak or read in class would cause her distress. She would physically react to stress with shakes, sweat, and by feeling lightheaded. Basinger is just one of a number of celebrities who live with anxiety; some will speak candidly about living with the disorder while others choose to not discuss their struggle.

Singer George Michael did not experience growing up with anxiety the way that Basinger did; rather he developed an anxiety disorder after nearly succumbing to pneumonia in November, 2011 (Fisher 2012). Michael says that doctors had warned him he might deal with post-traumatic stress disorder after what he'd gone through, but he thought if he went back to performing he could avoid this. In 2012 he was forced to cancel tour dates and seek treatment, admitting that he had been plagued by anxiety and panic attacks. Michael found that he did indeed need the post-traumatic counseling that his doctors had earlier recommended.

These public figures are exemplars of how anxiety can make itself known from a young age, or develop after a life-changing event. It is not a respecter of wealth or privilege. And no matter how hard someone works, there may be times when a person needs medical assistance to learn to live with their anxiety disorder. Perhaps the most important point to remember is that no matter the form that anxiety takes in a person's life, it does not have to be silently suffered. Treatment including counseling and medication can aid a person in learning to live with the impact anxiety has in their life. People can learn to manage these disorders; they may need support and encouragement to obtain the treatment needed to make managing feasible.

CHAPTER SEVEN

Affective/Mood Disorders

These are the disorders which impact a person's affect and mood: depression/unipolar disorder; bipolar disorder; the "milder" form of bipolar disorder, cyclothymia[1]; and schizophrenia. All these disorders are found amongst students, faculty, and staff on university campuses. These are also the disorders which arguably still have the greatest social stigma attached to them, a point that will be discussed later in this chapter.

Diagnostic classifications of mood disorders go on for many pages. At this point we will review just a handful of the most common mood disorders, providing an overview of what sets mood disorders apart from what most people will experience as part of an ordinary range of moods, i.e. "feeling blue" or "having a really bad day." These feelings, as well as being excited or irritated, are moods we all experience; remember, something becomes a disorder by exceeding normal feelings in duration and intensity. Everyone has a bad day—not everyone will struggle to get up and get dressed for weeks on end due to depression.

According to the National Institute of Mental Health (NIMH), *major depression* interferes with "a person's ability to work, sleep, study, eat, and enjoy once-pleasurable activities. Major depression is disabling and prevents a person from functioning normally" (NIMH 2011). A person may experience depression for shorter periods of time such as several weeks, or depression can last for months; obviously either will interfere with a person's ability to maintain routines such as studying, attending class, or working. Depression can also be reoccurring, for example, a person may find that they are suffering a clinical level of depression several times a year.

Bipolar disorder—sometimes called manic depression—is a cycle of manic [hyperactive/excitable] and depressive episodes [despondent to the point of suicidal]. There are different types of bipolar disorder (diagnostic criteria look at differences in duration and frequency of

---

1   The mood swings in cyclothymia are not as extreme as in type I or type II bipolar disorder.

manic and depressive episodes); what the different types of bipolar disorder have in common is this switching between mania and depression. As the NIMH pamphlet *Bipolar Disorder* explains, these changes in mood are accompanied by changes in behavior.

Behavioral changes during a manic episode include:

> Talking very fast, jumping from one idea to another, having racing thoughts, being easily distracted, increasing goal-directed activities such as taking on new projects, being restless, sleeping little, having an unrealistic belief in one's abilities, behaving impulsively and taking part in a lot of pleasurable, high-risk behaviors such as spending sprees, impulsive sex, and impulsive business investments. (NIMH 2008)

Behavioral changes during a depressive episode include:

> Feeling tired or slowed down; having problems concentrating, remembering, and making decisions; being restless or irritable; changing eating, sleeping, or other habits; thinking of death or suicide or attempting suicide. (NIMH 2008, p.2).

The length and frequency of episodes varies amongst individuals and some people will experience longer periods of moderate mood between episodes of either mania or depression. Others experience what is termed "rapid cycling" and as the name implies, move more frequently between extremes. As the pamphlet *Bipolar Disorder* points out, "Some people experience more than one episode in a week, or even within one day" (NIMH 2008, p.5). There seems to be a higher incident of rapid cycling amongst those who experience bipolar symptoms from a younger age and who live with a more severe form of the disorder (NIMH 2008, p.5). The pamphlet also reminds us that the disorder tends to become worse over time if not treated.

According to the NIMH, about 2.6 percent of American adults live with bipolar disorder—or 5.6 million people over the age of 18.[2] When other mood disorders, including major depression, are added together, however, then the NIMH estimates 26.2 percent of American adults are living with a mood disorder (NIMH 2013b).

Schizophrenia is a chronic disorder which is most likely to make itself known during a student's college years. The age of onset for

---

2   5.6 million based on 2004 census numbers (NIMH 2013c, "The numbers count"); the rate remains fairly constant and therefore the number of individuals affected will rise as the population increases.

schizophrenia is typically 16 to 30, which overlaps with the age when most people attend college; because teen behavior is expected to change from the behavior exhibited as a child, families may not realize their child is developing schizophrenia until their behavior begins to deteriorate in college (NIMH 2009). The National Health Service (NHS) outlines the following symptoms of schizophrenia:

- Hallucinations—hearing or seeing things that do not exist.

- Delusions—unusual beliefs, not based on reality, which often contradict the evidence.

- Muddled thoughts, based on the hallucinations or delusions.

- Changes in behavior.

(NHS 2012b)

The NHS and NIMH both report an incident rate of 1 in 100—or 1 percent of the population—living with schizophrenia.

For the remainder of this chapter we will focus primarily on bipolar disorder and schizophrenia; these have the greatest impact on the resources on campus, in part because they are the source for the greatest concern amongst the general public, who equate these disorders with "serious mental illness." As a society, we are less threatened by those suffering from major depression since these individuals are more likely to be withdrawn and quiet. While a student with major depression may use the campus counseling center, they are more likely to withdraw from classes or fail rather than have extensive interactions with campus faculty and staff. Popular media has yet to be filled with an outcry for educators to do a better job of tracking students with major depression, while there is increasing concern that not enough is done to "safeguard" students from their peers with bipolar disorder and schizophrenia (Coulter 2013; Fermier and Lang 2013).

Background

Emil Kraepelin (1856–1926) was the German psychiatrist who pioneered clinical studies of mental illness; his contemporary, Sigmund Freud, focused on psychoanalysis while Kraepelin focused on clinical observations of the mentally ill (Ebert and Bar 2010, p.191). Kraepelin appears to be the first to have noted the difference between schizophrenia and bipolar disorder. Previous to Kraepelin, mental illness was regarded as a range of behaviors, all called "psychosis."

Kraepelin actually used the terms "dementia praecox" and "manic depression" to divide mental illness into categories (his category of dementia praecox included more than schizophrenia). It was Swiss psychiatrist Eugen Bleuler who introduced the term schizophrenia in 1911 (Ebert and Bar 2010, p.192). Meanwhile, Kraepelin went on to write seminal early works on mental illness that would grow to become a multi-volume psychiatric textbook, part of which has been translated as *Manic Depressive Insanity and Paranoia* (translated: R. Mary Barclay, Kraepelin 1920). Kraepelin noted the "pressured speech" and rapid thought process which continue to be considered hallmarks of a manic episode (Kraepelin 1920, p.32). He also included photos of patients, so that clinicians would have examples of how a manic episode physically presented in different individuals. Examples he used included a woman placing her hair into a number of small braids (socially uncommon at the time) and a series of photos of the many physical gestures that were part of another patient's talking when she was in a manic episode. Kraepelin also documented how patients' weight and blood pressure would change during an extended period of depression and included photos of patients in the grip of depression. Kraepelin's observations continue to be echoed in DSM-V criteria for manic and depressive episodes; he accurately noted what are still considered to be clinically significant symptoms of the disorders.

Group identity

In his blog entry under *Healthy Living* on HuffPost, Mills Baker shares that he believes he has the persona of a bipolar person; he is creative and energetic, yet irritable, outgoing yet fickle (Baker 2012). He acknowledges that he can only speak for how he experiences bipolar disorder, that he has not known rapid-cycling (except as a side-effect of medication) and that he has, in the past, self-medicated with drinking. He also mentions, though, something that bipolar people have in common, particularly in a manic phase—the sense that somehow there is also a specialness that comes with being bipolar, an ability to be more intense, more creative and artistic than the general public. Baker suggests that this is an idealism that is supported by Western social views in which artists, including writers, musicians, painters and actors, have been held up for admiration for their tortured creative genius—which often is perceived as being part and parcel of their bipolar identity.

As Baker points out, the connection between "madness" and creativity has long been touted in Western society, probably as much by those who live with manic episodes as anyone. It has been *speculated* that many well-known creative people, including Virginia Woolf, Edgar Allan Poe, Mark Twain, Gauguin, O'Keeffe, Van Gogh, Charles Mingus, Beethoven, Schumann—even rock guitarist Jimi Hendrix—lived with the manic energy and crushing depression of bipolar disorder. This perceived connection between creativity and mental illness is not new; from Aristotle to current studies, there continue to be observations that what we now know as bipolar disorder seems to occur more often in the same "bloodlines" that are prone to a capacity to create (Andreasen 1987). It is also speculated that creative people, particularly writers, seem more prone to suicide and self-medication through drinking and drugs, also as a result of bipolar disorder and depression (Andreasen 1987).

Members of Stanford University's Department of Psychiatry and Behavioral Sciences have conducted studies to try and measure if in fact creativity and affective disorders seem to co-occur more often than does creativity in a "healthy" population (Santosa *et al.* 2006; Srivastava *et al.* 2010). Their studies continue to show that there is a higher incident of creativity in those with bipolar disorder; however, those who live with major depressive disorder do not seem to enjoy any greater capacity for creativity than the general population. Another noteworthy observation from the Stanford studies is how "creative" personality types "endorse" adjectives "such as clever, confident, humorous, informal, resourceful, snobbish, and unconventional" (Santosa *et al.* 2006, p.33). In other words, those of us in the arts have a propensity to self-identify as above average in intelligence, creativity, and humor. This forms a reinforcing loop of self-identity and social view; creative-means-different feeds into how both the individual and society view the propensity for creativity going hand in glove with mental/emotional struggles, with both society and the affected individual expecting this to be true.

Socially, it has long been more acceptable to appear eccentric if one is creatively prolific and/or successful. Those who work in fields outside the arts, however, are not known to be so quick to self-identify as bipolar to their co-workers or peers. Mental illness of any kind continues to be attached to negative social images. People tend not to realize how much of their "information" about mental illness is actually influenced not by facts but by popular media representations of those with mental illness in television and movies, or by sensationalized media reports in newspapers, magazines and on radio.

Studies have actually found that media portrayals of mental illness continue to reinforce negative, and inaccurate, messages about mental illness, with perhaps the most repeated theme being that those with mental illness are likely to be violent (Tartakovsky 2009). Seventy percent of respondents in an American study said they took their information about mental illness from TV news magazine shows; study results from Australia, Scotland, and Canada show that American citizens are not alone in learning what they "know" about mental illness based on what they see in popular media sources such as television and newspapers (Edney 2004). Just as these inaccurate depictions influence the larger society, they also influence those living with the disorder. People in professions outside the arts are reluctant to disclose that they live with a mental illness when they know others will equate their illness with a propensity for violence.

Ironically, the fact is those who live with mental illness are far more likely to be the victims of violence and crime than perpetrators (Eisenberg 2005; Teplin et al. 2005). Comparisons of incidents of crime between those with mental illness and the general population, found those with mental illness are 11 times more likely to be victims of a crime and four times more likely to be a victim of a violent crime than other members of the public. A study in Finland found that schizophrenic adults, in the three years they were followed after release from hospital for treatment, experienced a 5.6 percent rate of violent crime directed against them (Honkonen et al. 2004, p.606). During that same time period the rate of violent crime in Finland was 1.7 percent (Honkonen et al. 2004, p.610).

Society loses sight of the fact that the majority of people, with or without mental illness, do not commit violent crimes. When a violent crime is committed, as a society we posit that the person responsible must be socially deviant—"normal people" don't hurt each other being the dominant social view. Yet, the greatest predictor of violent crime is not the presence of mental illness, but of alcohol consumption (McClelland and Teplin 2001). In both Canada and the US studies report between a 42 percent to 53 percent of alcohol involvement in incidents of homicide (McClelland and Teplin 2001, p.71). According to statistics compiled by the US Department of Justice, when analyzing the results of crime reports from 1980–2008 (Cooper and Smith 2011), it was found that:

- 63.7 percent of murdered women were killed by someone they were intimate with; 81.7 percent of murdered women were killed in a sex-related homicide

- 56.4 percent of male murder victims were killed by someone they knew; 90 percent of those murders involved circumstances with drugs

- older victims of homicide are most likely to be killed while a felony is being committed (rape, robbery, arson)

- 57.7 percent of murders took place in cities with populations over 100,000; one-third of those cities had populations over one million.

Men are more likely than women to be murdered; people living in urban centers are more likely to be murdered than those in rural areas. Less than 1 percent of homicides in a year involve three or more victims (Cooper and Smith 2011, p.24)—such as mass shootings—yet these are obviously the types of murders which attract the greatest media attention and perhaps lead to speculation that mentally ill people are likely to murder people at a school. One is more likely to be murdered during the committal of a robbery or as a result of domestic violence than as a result of a mentally ill person's attack. This certainly is not the impression of society at large, doubtless as a result of the portrayal of mental illness and violence as seen in popular media. These negative stereotypes are likely one of the strongest influences which keep employees from sharing their disability status with employers. As mentioned earlier, all those who live with a disability would benefit from ongoing support; due to misinformation which leads to social prejudice, half of all employees with a disability feel they must keep their disability undisclosed. This is particularly true when the disability is a type of mental illness.

It is a sort of cold comfort to recognize one's own creative and/ or intellectual strengths while also feeling compelled to hide a large portion of one's identity from colleagues and peers. To disclose that one has a mental illness, though, is to risk being judged precarious, potentially dangerous or unreliable—none of which are sought-after attributes in a work environment. While self-identity can include an elevated opinion of one's capacity, the co-mingling of a propensity for despair and negative social image often has deadly results. Results show that amongst those who commit suicide, 90 percent have an "axis I" major mental disorder (Rihmer 2007). In the longest follow-up study done to date (34–38 years) it was found that people with a mood disorder averaged an 18 percent suicide rate (Angst *et al.* 2002); according to the National Alliance on Mental Illness (NAMI), 1.3 percent of all US deaths were from suicide (Pearson 1996).

Physiology

Bipolar disorder has a genetic component, although scientists are still working to identify exactly which sections of DNA are responsible for the disorder (Holmans *et al.* 2009). Schizophrenia also has a genetic component; studies suggest that there may in fact be genetic overlap in the sources of the two disorders and that they may prove to be on a shared continuum of genetic mutation as opposed to disorders with two separate causes (Holmans *et al.* 2009; Craddock, O'Donovan and Owen 2005).

Studies also indicate that genetics are more determinate in developing a mood disorder than is environment (Smoller and Finn 2003). Environmental factors, however, do play a role in the levels of stress and trauma a person is exposed to; it has been observed that there is a higher level of post-traumatic stress disorder (PTSD) amongst those with severe mental illness including schizophrenia than average (Mueser *et al.* 2002). A study of drinking habits amongst those with severe mental illness, schizophrenia, and PTSD found that this was a group with a higher rate of drinking than average due to the use of a "drink-to-cope" strategy (O'Hare and Sherrer 2011). The report suggests the reason for drinking—to cope with trauma—needs to be taken into account when providing treatment, particularly since while alcohol acts as a depressant, the study found it did successfully provide some relief from the acute stress experienced as part of PTSD. The report also recommends working with mentally ill clients on identifying "ways to cope more effectively" as a "primary focus of clinical care" (O'Hare and Sherrer 2011, p.468).

Comorbid disorders

AD/HD, anxiety disorder, obsessive compulsive disorder (OCD), PTSD, and migraines all have a high rate of comorbidity with bipolar disorder. One study found that 60 percent of bipolar patients had at least one comorbid disorder—one-quarter of bipolar patients had three or more additional disorders (Sasson *et al.* 2003). What might be more surprising is that people living with bipolar disorder are not just at risk for a greater range of physical complaints centered in the brain.

A Canadian cross-national study was designed to quantify to what extent people with bipolar disorder had comorbid health complaints (McIntyre *et al.* 2006). Data were taken from the *Canadian Community Health Survey* (McIntyre *et al.* 2006, p.1140). The findings included significantly higher than average rates for:

- asthma

- gastric ulcers

- chronic bronchitis

- multiple chemical sensitivity

- chronic fatigue syndrome.

(McIntyre *et al.* 2006, p.1142)

The rate of occurrence of these disorders was often almost twice that of the general population (e.g. asthma 15.9% in bipolar vs. 8.3% general population; gastric ulcer 10.8% vs. 3.9%). Those with bipolar disorder also had an observable, if not as significantly increased incident of other health conditions, e.g. arthritis (20.6% bipolar vs. 17.4% general population); thyroid; Crohn's disease; fibromyalgia (McIntyre et al. 2006, p.1142).

Schizophrenia also presents with a high rate of comorbidity for other psychiatric disorders including: panic disorder; PTSD; OCD; and depression (Buckley *et al.* 2009). Substance abuse due at least in part to self-medication is also common. Because schizophrenia can include auditory and visual hallucinations, it has been speculated that doctors may not take the complaints of physical ailments as seriously amongst schizophrenic patients, or may question what is a valid medical complaint from an "imagined" one (Jeste *et al.* 2006). When conducting an extensive review of literature, Jeste *et al.* found that research centered on schizophrenic patients had "consistently demonstrated deficits in learning" and pointed out this was significant; schizophrenic patients are often non-compliant with taking medication and the authors note that this may be at least in part due to "encoding and retrieval problems" that make it difficult for patients to understand, remember, and follow instructions regarding their medication (Jeste *et al.* 2006, p.422).

This study also found that schizophrenic patients were "eight times more likely [than the general public] to die from traumatic injuries" while approximately 10 percent would commit suicide (Jeste *et al.* 2006, p.416). The lifespan of someone who is schizophrenic is on average also ten years shorter than for others (Jeste *et al.* 2006, p.416). Jeste *et al.* concluded from their analysis that "These results suggest that schizophrenic patients may receive less than adequate healthcare" (Jeste *et al.* 2006, p.413). It is easy to see, given these statistics, why schizophrenic patients may fight their diagnosis—society still treats this as a "hopeless" disorder. It is important to realize that successful, professional people are able to manage schizophrenia with treatment—this will be discussed towards the end of the chapter. The reality is, schizophrenia does not keep people from being highly intelligent, high functioning, and very able to work. Like any disability, schizophrenia complicates daily functioning.

Presentation

The transition to college is a stressful time for all students. This is compounded by the fact that if a young person is a candidate for mental health conditions, the onset of these disorders is most likely to overlap with the time in their life when they start college. According to Hunt and Eisenberg, "Mental disorders account for nearly one-half of the disease burden for young adults in the United States" (Hunt and Eisenberg 2010, p.3). In reviewing the literature, Hunt and Eisenberg also relay that the American College Health Association reports that only 24 percent of students with a diagnosis of depression were in treatment while only 20 percent of those with anxiety disorder were being treated (Hunt and Eisenberg 2010, p.6). We will revisit this concern in Chapter Ten when discussing policies; this study also points out how overwhelmed campus counseling facilities tend to be. Given the increasing number of students in need of counseling services, there certainly are implications for how funding and staffing of counseling centers needs to be part of planning at an administrative level.

Mick *et al.*'s study found that children with bipolar disorder tended to rank higher in problems with attention, aggression, and anxiety (Mick *et al.* 2003, p.1025). They are also irritable with a high comorbidity of attention deficit disorder. Irritability and anxiety are two factors that are likely to be present in college age students, as is a notable level of struggling with attention. Faculty and staff may wonder if a person is living with bipolar disorder or attention deficit disorder when encountering someone who struggles with attention and anxiety issues. The actual label is less important than is understanding the type of support that will help the person to function.

Support

Allowance for notes that provide guidelines – such as bullet points/ outlines – can be useful for those with anxiety issues and attention issues; stress is reduced when there are reminders that can be referred back to, particularly if someone isn't sure they caught a point correctly the first time through. Reminders and multiple ways of giving the same information – written, verbally, slides or overheads – also allow students to review and reassure themselves that they are keeping track of the correct main points, including due dates. Again, because there are significant overlaps between mental illness, anxiety, language processing and attention disorders, some of the same supports are helpful to all students. Multiple formats of presenting similar information is useful for most students/workers.

Those with mood disorders are also likely living with other comorbid disorders which may complicate their health. Flexibility in work/study environments, including negotiable deadlines when possible, can be very useful. When living with mental illness, there will be days when even the highest functioning individual will need to take a day off; allowing for work to be made up and for occasional sick days is important when dealing with students, faculty and staff, as mental illness is to be found amongst individuals in each of these groups. High functioning people with mental health issues – and those who arrive at university are high functioning – have considerable intellect and creativity to offer society and are often very dedicated workers, as work helps keep their minds occupied. Allowing for the flexibility these people need to be successful can meet a profitable return in keeping individuals who are dedicated to their work/study affiliated with the same institution.

It is also important to recognize that a person who has not already been displaying signs of mental illness is most likely to begin showing impacts of the disability at young adult age and during the stress of transitioning to college or their first significant job. Employers and institutions can be most proactive by providing access to mental healthcare services with free or low-cost counseling services and to mental healthcare professionals. Those who are able to seek treatment without fear of reprisal or negative impact on their employment or school record are those most likely to maintain their mental health. With the widespread incident of depression and anxiety, it behoves an institution to make certain that mental healthcare is readily available. Society is best served by assisting all of us in maintaining mental health, rather than trying to foresee which of us is most likely to act out when mental health support is not readily available.

Public figures

Elyn R. Saks has a genius grant from the MacArthur Foundation, she is a chaired fellow at the University of Southern California Gould School of Law, and is on the faculty of both the New Center for Psychoanalysis and the psychiatric department of the medical school at the University of California (Saks 2013). She and her colleagues have been conducting ground-breaking research on schizophrenia amongst college students. Professor Saks was motivated in this research in part because when she was diagnosed with schizophrenia 30 years ago she was told her future would be in a group home and if she was lucky, she could hope to work in menial jobs. Her current study includes 20 men and women, who are professionals, including doctors, lawyers, and managers. Their average age is 40, they are all schizophrenic and some of the keys to their success include: medication, therapy, controlling sensory input, spirituality, and work. Having work/studies to focus on allows them to feel useful and helps them keep other symptoms of their psychosis at bay. Professor Saks suggests that focusing on what an individual can do, where their personal strengths are, and offering treatment that allows people to continue to function in the work environment is more productive for society and the individual.

Singer Sinead O'Connor has been open about living with both bipolar disorder and post-traumatic stress disorder. She has also shared that when her medical concerns are not considered when plans are made for her working and performing life, she eventually reaches the point where she has to withdraw and regroup. She states that she fired her business manager because while he did very well with the business side of things, he continued to ignore the impact that overbooking her for performances had on her mental health (Pittman 2012).

Harry Potter creator J.K. Rowling has also been open about her experience with clinical depression, which she discussed during the making of a documentary that followed her life for a year (Rowling 2007). Rowling admits that she was so depressed, she woke every morning expecting to find that her young daughter had died; she explains that everything in her life seemed so bleak that she just expected to lose her beloved child as well. Her experience with depression inspired her creation of the Dementors in the Harry Potter series. Her description of Dementors does a fair job of giving insight into what an episode of major depression is like; something which all those who live with a mood disorder will experience multiple times in their lives:

> Dementors are among the foulest creatures that walk this earth. They infest the darkest, filthiest places, they glory in decay and despair, they drain peace, hope, and happiness out of the air around them... Get too near a Dementor and every good feeling, every happy memory will be sucked out of you. If it can, the Dementor will feed on you long enough to reduce you to something like itself...soulless and evil. You will be left with nothing but the worst experiences of your life. (Rowling 2001, p.187).

Given that those with mood disorders all deal with this soul-sucking depression at least some time—while others battle it their entire life—may be helpful in understanding why some days a person with a mood disorder needs quiet time alone, or to lose themselves in activities which take their mind elsewhere. Some people find escape in reading or writing, others in television or music, and some in physical activity. Many, however, learn to focus on their work and can be very productive employees precisely because the more absorbed they are in work, or studies, the less likely it is that they will be overwhelmed with despair.

CHAPTER EIGHT

Universal Design and Lecture Hall Based Classes

The concept of designing products and spaces so that the largest range of consumers possible could use them began in architecture, but has successfully spread to a wide range of fields for a simple reason—it is a very useful concept. When a building, classroom, or assignment is designed from the onset so that the largest number of people possible are accommodated, we no longer need to spend as much time or as many resources re-designing and re-planning to include those who were excluded by the original design.

Architect Ronald Mace coined the term *universal design*; in his work Mace always explicated the background and historical changes which led to the need and practicality of the work he was doing (The Center for Universal Design 2008; The RL Mace Universal Design Institute 1998). Mace used the following facts when explaining the necessity of designing usable spaces:

- People are living later into life—many develop limits, or disabilities, as part of the aging process.

- Medicine/medical treatment allow people to survive injuries and illness that used to be fatal—they often survive with a disability.

- Laws are changing, requiring builders to make buildings accessible—making a building accessible "after the fact" decreases the esthetic value of a space.

- Society is changing—civil rights movements now include the disabled, who want equal access to places and opportunities.

- The number of people identified as disabled has increased— approximately 20 percent of the US population for example now has some level of disability, with almost 10 percent having a "severe" disability.

(The RL Mace Universal Design Institute 1998)

Universal design is basically an elegant solution to the architectural dilemma—how do we design this space to be usable by as wide a range of users as possible; design from the beginning, so that the elements of design take usability into account.

Other fields had also considered the issue of making/producing items that would work well for those who would be using them, but usually in a more limited way than universal design imagines the user. *User testing* is the practice of not considering a design finished until it has been tried by a sample group of users, then modified in response to user feedback. Universal design in effect says, when considering your group of "sample users" you must consider the range of people who make up the public, not just the able-bodied, or the young, or the physically fit. Before universal design, the group of potential users was usually much more narrowly defined and "able-bodied" was a default assumption. Designers and producers were often simply designing for users who were like themselves. When one is able-bodied it is often taken for granted the kind of access that being able-bodied allows, for example, if one is able to use steps, and uses steps frequently, one may never stop to consider that steps can present a barrier to others. Universal design requires builders, producers, and other makers to be much more conscious of the range of people who could potentially make up the group of "users" of their product or space.

Transitioning to universal

For educators and educational institutions, there have been significant changes among two populations: students and employees. It is no longer reasonable to assume that students will be limited to able-bodied youth, straight out of high school, who will complete degrees in four years and have families who will contribute significantly to their financial needs. For employers it is no longer safe to assume able-bodied employees who will stay with the same institution for their entire career—or that gender stereotypes and gender roles remain the same, i.e. women working as "auxiliary" income earners to their husbands, or heterosexual couples, or families who share benefits through marriage. Yet many of our policies, procedures and physical spaces are carry overs from a time when these were the dominant assumptions.

In the remainder of this book we will examine how changes in the disability status of students and employees impacts the educational process and institution. What follows in this chapter will be consideration of how the lecture-hall based class and space is affected when we consider changes amongst students. Chapter Nine will consider the impact on the smaller classes and classroom spaces resulting from changes amongst students, while Chapter Ten will analyze the influence and considerations on policies and procedures within the institution based on changes amongst students and employees—both faculty and staff.

Enriched environments

We have established in the preceding chapters that due to a range of disabilities and overlaps in disabilities, most learners are well served when information in the classroom is presented in more than one format—or modality. *Multiple modalities*—or multiple formats (aural, visual, tactile) used to present information increase the likelihood that a range of learners will be able to access what is being taught in the classroom.

Multi-modality has challenges based on the size of space and number of users in a space where communication is taking place. A lecture hall can seat anything from 100 to several hundred students at once; some lecture halls hold upwards of 1500 students at a time. Given what we now know about the level of anxiety, stress, and trouble focusing that many students live with, we can now see why lecture halls provide specific problems for many students and professors, who may also be disabled. The number of people present create a background buzz of noise, there will always be someone moving or otherwise providing distraction, and simply being in such a crowded space can increase anxiety for many people. How professors will be accommodated is often a matter of policy (Chapter Ten); at this point we will review some of the ways that professors can make the material covered in class accessible to a wider range of people. Some of the multi-modal possibilities a teacher can use in a lecture class include:

- **Microphones**—when a professor uses a microphone, it allows people throughout a large room to hear what is being said and increases the strength of the professor's voice; students who have trouble focusing are better able to focus on the "main" voice in class when it is amplified.

- **Large screens**—can be placed at the front of the classroom, and sometimes along the sides of a lecture hall, so that students are better able to see what is being presented at the front of the room.

- **PowerPoint, video, and other visual media**—can be projected onto the screens, providing the key points of information in an additional format to that of voice. This can be very important for those students who rely primarily on visual learning.

- **Computers**—in classrooms where students are able to bring in laptop computers, or where computers can be provided, students have an additional way of processing information. Typing can allow students who struggle to write to take notes, and to take notes they can read. Word processing with a computer also incorporates another modality in learning.

  Teachers can use computers and programs to design original presentations and content which demonstrate a point, concept, or to present an example in a way that clarifies what is being taught. Computers allow for more sophisticated examples than a board and piece of chalk have allowed.

  It is also possible to project content such as web pages onto large screens. In this way, for example, a professor could show students in chemistry classes a chemical reaction that's taken place in the laboratory, stopping the footage at different points to make unique stages of the reaction more evident. There are few limits outside a professor's imagination to the kind of examples that can be shown in class this way. Seeing the "live" example will teach students in a different way than lecturing on a principle is able to; it also allows a teacher to show how principles are put into practice.

- **Projected white-board content**—in lecture halls it is becoming more commonplace to have a "white-board" at the front of the class, where the teacher can write information that is then projected onto the screens in class. Using these boards in conjunction with a lecture can replace using a chalk-board.

White-boards are actually easier than chalk-boards for those with a range of vision and learning disabilities to see; the projected written material can also be seen in more seats in the class, rather than just from the seats near the front of the room. And with colored markers, a teacher can make a more visible distinction between key ideas, for example, making different lines/angles more distinct through a use of different colors.

- **Small lab sections**—because some students will always learn best through hands-on interaction, ideally large lecture classes will whenever possible incorporate smaller laboratory sections that allow students hands-on practice of material. Labs can also incorporate modalities of learning that a lecture class is unable to—such as question and answer time—and augment the material that is presented in class. Labs also allow students to put principles into practice.

Multi-modality should be considered not just when presenting students with information; multi-modality should also be a consideration in how students are allowed to show what they have learned. Typically a large lecture will have one way of grading students—exams which use computer-processed answer sheets. Students respond to the test questions by using a pencil to fill in the small bubbles on the answer sheet and the answer sheet is then fed through a computer to be graded.

When a student has their grade based on just several such exams, then many students will be penalized for their inability to focus or because they find such environments tremendously stressful. It is also anxiety producing to know that one's grade is based on just several such exams, particularly if one is aware that such exams typically do not allow him or her to accurately show what they have learned. Anxiety is increased by placing a person in a context where they have an increased fear of failure due to previous failure in a similar context. Professors often despair, though, that there is simply no other practical way to have students in such large lecture classes show they have learned information.

There are at least a few options, however, that are being successfully used in some lecture classes to increase modality for the learners, or at least to assist students in managing their stress by increasing the number of times and ways the student has to be successful in the class:

- Whenever possible, incorporate a laboratory section into the class and have the work done in the laboratory count as a significant portion of the lecture-class grade (worth as much as at least one exam).

- Design exams to take only half the available test time, then allow the entire class the equivalent of "double time" to write the exam (this reduces stress for many students, including those who may silently live with an anxiety disorder).

- Give at least four tests during the course of the semester and divide the grade equally among all the tests so no one test carries more weight, or stress, than any other.

- Give at least five tests, and allow students to drop the lowest grade.

- Provide computer-based homework that allows students to practice working with concepts and receive feedback from the computer program regarding what they are doing correctly and where they still need to practice (there are an increasing range of computer-based programs available).

- Implement (or design an original computer program) that allows students to interactively review key concepts and take mini-tests.

- Allow students multiple attempts to retake online test and homework so that they continue to improve their retention of the information—practice and revision provide both lower-risk learning opportunities and increased retention of information.

It has been observed that the best way to learn something is to try and teach it to others. Some lecture classes are small enough that students can be divided into groups and each group can be given an opportunity to give a presentation about a key idea to the class, designing their own questions for the class and creating opportunities for question and answer periods at the end of their presentation. Multi-modal classroom design means that opportunities are created to let as wide a range of learners as possible show what they have learned; some students will be uncomfortable with group work, others with reading, others with speaking, while others will struggle to sit still in class. By providing variety in the way students can earn their grade, a teacher creates a more universal learning experience—everyone should have at least one opportunity in the semester to excel at doing something that falls within their strength-set, rather than being limited to being graded on activities that emphasize their disability.

There is now an online source for detailed information for educators interested in learning more about universal design—the *National Center on Universal Design for Learning* provides many pages of information that can be referenced for educators and community members who are interested in learning more: www.udlcenter.org. While the site is primarily focused on teachers in the kindergarten to grade 12 school system, the concepts are foundational to teaching in general. For example, the Center breaks learning into three categories based on how the brain works:

1. Recognition networks—How we gather facts and categorize what we see, hear, and read.

2. Strategic networks—Planning and performing tasks. How we organize and express our ideas.

3. Affective networks—How learners get engaged and stay motivated (The National Center on Universal Design for Learning 2011).

An example of how this is applied to teaching in a lecture hall environment will follow in the next section on teaching practices. These three networks—recognition, strategic, affective—underlie the pedagogical reasons for suggestions being made herein, as will be explained.

There are also online sites dedicated to instruction at the university level; interestingly, these sites often spend more time on theory than on actual suggestions for how to put universal design into practice. None-the-less, they can be very useful as starting points for discussions. It would be a useful practice for those within a field of study to discuss together the concepts and principles behind universal design and work on ideas for how to better implement the theory in practice in the classes they teach. The most useful ideas are likely to come from exchanges of "best practices" between those with similar teaching demands.

Teaching practices

What makes for a "large" or "small" class varies considerably based on one's context, i.e. schools range from student bodies of 2000 to schools with over 30,000, and what will mean "large" in each context will vary considerably. Introductory classes that most or all students are required to take are the classes most often taught in lecture halls. These classes might include introductory chemistry, biology, math, and some of the humanity/social science "survey" courses. The idea is to provide a large number of students with the same foundational information at the same time. Lecture classes are also the classes which tend to put most students at a disadvantage; only a minority of learners identify sitting and listening to a person speak as their ideal way to learn.

Professors can use technology-rich environments—rooms where there is audio-visual recording possible for example—to record their entire lecture and make it available online. This allows students to review, stop, and replay the class after the fact. It also makes the information more accessible to those whose anxiety is severe enough that attending class in person handicaps their ability to learn. When going *online* this way, a professor can still choose to limit the content availability to just those with a password, or they can choose to post their information so that it is *open-content*, i.e. anyone who chooses to can view. All colleges and universities now employ people whose role is to support faculty and staff in using technology; these technical staff as well as colleagues (and students) who are more versed in internet applications can assist professors in taking their class content online.

Requiring students to be physically present in class where, due to the number of students within the class, it is not possible for students to ask questions, seems of limited value. There are some students who are best served by being physically present in the room with the professor and other students—the energy in the room will help them absorb ideas in a way that watching a computer screen may not. For other students, however, being present in large lecture halls serves no practical purpose as they are too anxious or distracted to hear or learn anything that is happening. For students who, due to anxiety or distraction, are simply not able to learn by being present in a lecture hall, online content is a boon to becoming educated.

Another option that does not necessarily make the class available at any time for viewing, is to *live stream* the class while it is being taught. In this case audio-visual equipment and computers are used to make the lecture available in real time, i.e. as it is happening. This has been used to a limited extent with audio-visual equipment and television—in some cases students would even gather in a room to view the same televised content as part of a *distant education* classroom. Computer technology no longer requires students to gather in a central room and is therefore much more flexible. A disabled student can remain in their own room/home and view the content without a need to travel (as arguably any student can). As an educator I do see a difference, however, in making content available online for those with disabilities versus obtaining all of one's education in an online environment. Consider that for some disabled individuals education will be a matter of maintaining their quality of life: their aim is not necessarily to become qualified to work in a field that would require them to put skills like working with others into practice. At the same time, a person's discomfort in being in a lecture hall does not mean they cannot find meaningful employment in a work environment; many work environments do not require people to work in groups of several hundred or a thousand people in one room at one time. As an educator I also see a difference in not being able to manage the anxiety related to being in a large lecture hall full of people, and not being able to attend a small class. Students who are not ready for any social interaction with others are generally not prepared for a work environment; I see at least a qualitative difference between not being able to attend smaller discussion/seminar based classes and laboratories, and not being able to attend large lecture classes. We know that environments and ecosystems have tipping points beyond which they cannot maintain life—it makes sense that individuals will also have tipping points beyond which they cannot maintain learning in environments that over-stress their brain's sensory response.

Remember from the preceding section that there are three aspects of how our brain's neural processing works that impacts how we learn. *Recognition networks* impact how we gather facts and categorize what we see, hear, and read. Presenting information in different ways—in class, through lecture, through multi-modal media, through laboratory work with hands-on learning and practice, through discussion and presentations—these all allow the brain to develop recognition networks so that the information being learned is remembered.

Strategic networks affect our planning and performing of tasks. When students are allowed multiple ways to show what they have learned, this allows their brain to organize and express ideas in a range of ways; since some brains are impaired in some areas that would impact where and how information is stored, being able to show knowledge in different ways increases the likelihood that each student will have at least one method of showing they have learned without having to focus on an impaired region of their brain. Rather than using just two exams and basing an entire semester's grade on those two exams (making them "high-risk" assignments), using multiple, equally weighted exams, laboratory assignments, homework, and opportunities to revise and practice, increases the likelihood that students will be able to both initially encode the information and later be able to recall the information their brain has encoded.

Affective networks affect how learners, and their brains, get engaged and stay motivated. What motivates a student and keeps him or her engaged in a topic will obviously vary from student to student. Some will be excited by carrying out experiments, some by field work, by presenting, discussion, writing, or working with peers. Some students get excited by ideas while others need to take part in actual work to feel motivated. Ironically, grades are often considered a student's "primary motivation"; however, the concept of getting a good grade does not necessarily have any impact on a brain's affective network. A compelling demonstration or lab experiment on the other hand, might excite an otherwise disengaged student.

The more ways a teacher can find to engage a student in what is being taught, the more likely the student's brain is to hold onto the information it is being exposed to. The more ways we allow students to show us what they are learning, the more likely we are to get an accurate idea of what they have learned, rather than finding out the limits their disability imposes on them in one particular environment. The more ways a student can interact with new knowledge, the more likely he is to care about what he's learning, and thus, the more likely he is to actually learn.

Administrative considerations

How often do departments consider their broad survey courses fit with the potential to draw in students to their field of study? Too often these entry level survey courses are approached as onerous, the obligatory offerings that stand between a teaching professor and the opportunity to teach upper level classes. While there is usually competition to teach upper level classes and graduate seminars, the crowded entry level survey courses are currently undervalued by teachers. I would suggest that this undervaluing is a mirror of the undervaluing that administratively is shown towards these classes.

Consider the different approach that teaching these classes would take if they became administratively valued classes. What if teachers of these large survey classes were given credit for 1.5 or 2 times the teaching load of a smaller class? What if rather than seniority, or lack of it, those given priority for these teaching spots was decided based on how engaged in the class students reported being—what if positive student evaluations were used as a basis for assigning survey classes, and teachers of these classes were given extra credit towards their teaching load? How much more motivated to teach a class would a professor be, if the work that went into teaching an *engaging large class* was recognized in a way that professors value? This might also include as counting as extra teaching time when considering who is eligible for a sabbatical, or releases from teaching for part of a semester. Alternatively, teachers with the skills to make these large classes engaging to a range of students could be given bonuses. How can one's department show faculty—and students—that these large classes are valued by the department, that the learning of students in these classes is also valued, and that professors who can teach these classes well will be rewarded? How significant a change might take place in the tone of the institution if students felt from their first entry level classes that the institution, the department, and the professor were all supporting student success from the beginning of their college career, by making knowledge as accessible as possible?

CHAPTER NINE

Universal Design in the Smaller Classroom

My experience in education includes 14 years teaching at the university level with my very first teaching assignment being particularly challenging. The class I was assigned had one of the more "complex" mandates I've yet encountered. This was a mandatory class, one that all students were required to take. It was a mix of English, history, and art appreciation, housed in the Humanities Department. Topics to be covered included: the history of the US from inception to the 1960s; several significant artists and artistic movements, including the Harlem Renaissance; instruction on better writing, including how to write a strong, basic essay and a longer research paper; and coverage of two novels—one of which was *The Great Gatsby*. Needless to say, this was a course that was neither popular with students, or particularly straightforward to teach, particularly since most of the topics covered deserved an entire course in and of themselves. Challenges were added by the fact that the class was designed to be taught in lecture style with once a week labs where the teacher met with sections made up of half the class.

This class was also an awkward size—a little large for a regular class, but not as large as most lecture hall classes—60 students were in each class; the lab sections were 30 students each. Classroom space itself varied. Sometimes one would get lucky and have a class with tables and movable chairs; however, it was more common to either have standard lecture halls where the chairs were attached to the floor, or rooms full of small, older desks, with the "table" section built into the chair—in other words, one size was supposed to fit all. Neither the number of people, nor the seating was conducive to a diverse range of learners. Interestingly, given these challenges, many of us teaching the class rose to the occasion and did some of our best teaching in these environments. Instructors of this class won teaching awards and student comments often expressed that students felt this was one class where teachers knew them, cared about their learning, and where they felt their writing actually improved. I can also observe that most of us were very new in our teaching careers and that we were not experienced enough to realize all the reasons why what we were trying to do probably should not work.

We were also given two very important supports for this class. First, we all went through a *unified training* for one week before the semester started. At the time we complained bitterly that we were given too much information at once, that one week was not sufficient or that one week was too impossibly long—in hindsight we were blessed to have that week of reviewing material, designing assignments, and creating syllabi. We were also fortunate in that the most successful people already teaching the class would give presentations on the assignments they had found most successful for each content area of the semester—*ideas for instruction and successful assignments were generously shared.*

Also, this opportunity to share continued throughout the semester. There were usually 40–60 sections of this class, and thus of teachers for this class, each semester (instructors were seldom given more than one section of the class to teach as the grading and preparation demands on time were so heavy). We teachers were divided into *mentored groups* of five or six each, given a senior professor as a mentor, and had weekly meetings where we discussed in more detail how to approach the upcoming section of material, how to deal with challenges in the classroom, including student conduct, and grading.

One of the valid complaints that can be made about those of us who are teaching professors is that unlike those who teach in the kindergarten to grade 12 system, those of us who teach at the post-secondary level seldom have teaching qualifications. We theoretically learn to teach by observing those who have taught us. In my opinion, analytical, mentored teaching which makes use of give and take of ideas is much more effective in creating professors who teach. What generally happens, though, is that professors copy teaching behavior they have seen from their own professors, without necessarily considering if the behavior is effective in creating an environment where learning can take place. A course in pedagogical purpose in the classroom can also be very useful for professors; minus that, there should be conversations amongst colleagues from time to time about what the purpose of assignments are and how to create assignments that better fulfill the teaching purpose within a class. For example, I have met more than one professor who seems to think timing people during testing in and of itself has value—yet they cannot defend this viewpoint pedagogically as useful in their field. The reality is that those in the working world are seldom put in situations where they must be able to recall information under timed conditions. The one notable exception is a field like surgery, where one must know exactly what to do without checking a reference. Most people in a work setting are often able to use reference material. It simply isn't necessary to memorize everything or to be able to recall facts under timed conditions.

For most fields of study, a test is an artificial context that is necessary in college but not in the later work world. The purpose of a test is to allow a professor to attempt to gauge how much students are learning. Unfortunately, tests are often gauging how long someone remains too distressed to recall what they do know, particularly when they are under a strict time constraint and/or in large rooms of people providing distractions and an increased sense of anxiety. The idea that we are recreating the stress of the work world in a test environment is rather ridiculous. Doing hands-on work in an area that one is passionate about has little to do with sitting in a room with a clock ticking away as someone monitors one's moves, looking for signs that one may be cheating. I personally work in a very stressful environment at times and my supervisor is seldom within eyesight or hearing, no one is timing me, and my "success or failure" has most to do with the level of engagement I am able to generate with the person or family I am working with in the moment. While I do well with such meetings and with public speaking, in my life there has been more than one occasion where my brain froze and I could not recall information that I could recall both before and after being in the testing environment. My inability to test well at times has nothing to do with my ability to perform my work and I believe I am in not unique in this—yet I continue to meet teachers who believe that the stress of testing is very similar to the stress of working. I have yet to see any data or studies that support this viewpoint; people who otherwise pride themselves on being very logically and scientifically driven continue to spout this belief as if there is copious data supporting their view. *Timed tests were developed to suit academic needs, not to accurately reflect working-world considerations.* Classrooms are booked throughout a day and bodies need to be moved in and out of rooms on schedules. Given these institutional restraints, often the best a teacher can do is to plan tests to require half the available test time, and in effect allow all students double time for the test—and announce this so that students have at least a somewhat reduced sense of anxiety regarding the test time and can focus better on the material.

Class format

Regardless of whether one is teaching in a lecture hall or in a more intimate seminar setting, the brain's networks and neural paths for learning have the same requirements as discussed in Chapter Eight. Neural pathways rely on recognition networks, strategic networks, and affective networks to take information in, code it, sort it, and to either engage a student or leave them staring blank-eyed. Providing multimodal ways for information to be taken in and for students to be engaged is an important part of providing learning opportunities for a range of learners. At this point I can virtually hear some of my teaching colleagues complaining, "You're making professors responsible for creating entertaining environments while students are an audience." This is to misunderstand what I am saying.

Teachers are responsible for creating learning environments that have the potential to engage a range of learners; students are responsible for attempting to take part, carrying out the given assignments to the best of their individual capacity, and for being present. Students are responsible for seeking professors out during office hours, when their questions are not clarified in class. Students are responsible for continuing to try, even when their first attempts are not successful. Students share responsibility with the teacher in maintaining open communication regarding class-related topics and work. The original task of making the topic in some way engaging, however, rests with the person responsible for creating the learning environment—the teacher. Since so many university teachers have not been formally taught how to teach, creating an engaging learning environment can be challenging. In learning how to teach I benefited from experienced mentors who shared insights and wisdom and who were good at engaging students, from sharing assignment ideas that others had already found successful, from discussions with other teachers regarding their own best practices, and from several classes about how to pedagogically design a class so that one created assignments and lessons that had a purpose in line with the term goals for the class. I also have had numerous discussions with teaching peers about the best and worst practices we saw amongst our own professors when we were students. We regularly discussed what worked and what did not work in engaging us as students. If one only considers this question as an individual, "What worked for me as a student"—then one is in danger of creating an class environment that only works for students who learn in a fashion similar to oneself. It is important to have this discussion with people who have a range of learning styles, so that when one designs their classroom activities, they do so in a way that allows for a range of learners (or "multiple users") to take part in some aspect of the class. Remember, each activity is likely to include some and exclude others, so it is important to try and create a range that allows students at least one opportunity to be included.

I will use this humanities class with the range of topics as an example, because it did incorporate topics more widespread than a class usually would; this may sound like an unfair advantage, but the truth was, no student wanted to be in the class, they all resented having to take the class, and as a result as teachers we began with a hostile audience. Getting people engaged in any aspect of the class was challenging, which is what makes this class a good example of a difficult class to teach or get students involved in. We designed and taught this class in ways that made use of the three neural networks that are involved in students' learning.

Recognition networks require that information be presented in multiple ways to increase the likelihood that each student in the room will encounter at least one way of processing the information so that it becomes memorable for their brain. It was common in this class to incorporate physical movement in the room—both the teacher's and students'. Yes, this could be very challenging and we'll consider examples of how this worked later. The purpose of the movement and the activities that accompanied it was to create multiple ways for the *strategic networks* of the brain to work with the content of the class, another way to support the brain's encoding of information so that it could later be retrieved. While changing activities in the class might support strategic networks, unpredictable activity can be very stressful for anxious students. *Affective networks* require students to be able to become engaged, meaning ideally they will not become too distressed or anxious to eventually participate in learning. Most teachers of this class found the best way to create a non-threatening class environment was (1) to begin the very first class with a discussion of the importance of being respectful to differing points of view; and (2) having a broad routine that the class followed, so that students had a sense they knew what to expect. Routine and low-risk assignments were foundational to supporting the context where learning could take place.

For example, the way I taught, the class would begin with me arriving early enough to talk to any students who also arrived a little early, while I also would write an outline of the day's main activities on one of the chalk-boards—this was before white-boards or computers in classrooms were commonplace. At the bottom of the day's list of activities, I would write reminders of any assignments that were coming due, providing *repetition* of due dates, as students were also given handouts with the assignment's guidelines and due dates. I had already observed that many of the students I was working with benefited from repetition of information and access to the same information in multiple formats. I didn't have the vocabulary at the time but I was working with multiple *recognition networks* within the students' brains.

Once class started, I would read and explain what was written on the board—providing multi-modal ways for students to gain the information (visually and aurally). This reinforced the information for different neural pathways. I would then spend 15–20 minutes covering the key points of information that needed to be covered during that class period. This was part of our *routine*—students knew what to expect and knew what they would be doing at each stage of a typical class. While doing this I would *write key words on the board* and then talk about the ideas behind these key words while walking around the room trying to *make eye contact with students around the room*—people who have difficulty with attention often found it easier to focus on me at least briefly when I was in their area of the room and/or looking at them. I would try to incorporate several questions into this section of the class, allowing students an *opportunity to speak*—which also provided another attention-grabbing moment for students with attention difficulties, while also engaging all three of the brain's networks previously mentioned.

I would then do something that is very difficult in a lecture hall, particularly in the halls where the desks were literally screwed into the floor. I would have specific questions or topic points for students to discuss, and have them *work in small groups* to discuss these points. I would allow them to *get out of their seats*, to stand, to sit on the floor, to move and to talk. I would give them a *specific set time*—usually five to eight minutes—and a very particular mandate; as a group they needed to discuss and answer a question, have a spokesperson ready, and when the class came back together as a whole, present their resolution of the question to the entire class.

We would also make use of the chalk-boards in the class. Knowing that some students were loath to talk in front of a large group, I frequently *provided opportunities for groups to write short responses on the chalk-board*; one person could write, another person could explain what was written to the class. Again, this engaged the students in multiple modalities, and provided opportunities for movement—something which the restless students always appreciated. To recap the broader outline of a class: Review assignments and the day's agenda; large class discussion and introduction of main points; small group discussion of assigned points; class comes back together to review the small groups' findings. No one activity lasted for more than 20 minutes. The pace and type of involvement required of students shifted at least twice during the class. The students had a fair idea of what was expected of them at the different points of class. With the comfort of the routine it was easier to ask students to stretch themselves when it came to discussing topics that perhaps were uncomfortable or at least unfamiliar. Since students could also write, work together, or choose to speak there was also flexibility for different ways of expressing and exploring ideas.

Classes ended with either groups still reporting in—sometimes they were so excited by ideas that students would debate points as others raised them—other times there would be a question/answer time where students wanted more information from me. As students became comfortable and felt safe in the environment these Q & A times usually become larger class discussions. Students were also responsible for teaching each other something each class, increasing the probability that everyone would walk out knowing at least the point they had presented to the rest of the class by the end of the class. Some students were more likely to dominate in larger class discussions, while otherwise quieter students were more likely to share in smaller group discussions. Shy students felt safe writing on the board because there were always multiple people up and writing at once; no one person had to be self-conscious that all eyes could be on them.

Another piece of making this format work was *learning student names*, a very real challenge for me and something I do not excel at the way many of my colleagues do. I could sometimes make up for my lack of ability to quickly and accurately recall names by *making eye contact* and speaking to a student. The point is, when a teacher interacts directly with a student by using their name or at least speaking directly to them while looking at them, the student is both more likely to respond and to feel they have been engaged in a conversation. Students who are engaged are more likely to feel that a teacher knows them and is interested in what they think—a huge motivating factor for a surprising number of students. What I lacked in name-recall, I somewhat made up for in my ability to sense when a student had an idea they wanted to share and when they would prefer to not speak in class on a particular topic. My personal teaching ethos is to never embarrass a student unless they are behaving disrespectfully, and I know that calling on someone who does not wish to be called on can be very embarrassing for the individual, particularly if they are already struggling with anxiety. As students learned to trust me as a teacher over the course of a semester, it became "safer" for them to respond when I would directly ask them what their thought on a question or point being discussed in class was. As a result, by the end of the semester even shy and otherwise quiet students were much more likely to volunteer to share an idea in class. Again, the more voices, points of view, and ways of considering an idea that are presented in a class, the more engaging and multi-modal the class becomes.

Not all teachers would be comfortable in a classroom where students are up, moving, and somewhat noisily discussing ideas. I found that I could keep the activity and noise level within reason by walking from group to group, checking in with each group as they discussed, and asking for a synopsis of what they were saying. Eye contact and physical proximity always allowed me to feel that while the class might seem a bit loud to someone walking by, it was reasonable and productive noise. I did not create this method of teaching—I learned it from other teachers. As teachers we discussed the pedagogical purpose of using larger and smaller groups and of changing the type of activities students did in order to keep students engaged.

Teacher engagement

I once had a professor in a math class who, like me, was not good at remembering names. He incorporated a *bonus-point project* from the beginning of the semester. Students could earn these bonus-points by providing him with a picture of themselves attached to a standard-sized filing card with their name and a fact about themselves clearly written on the card. At the beginning of every class he would quickly go through the cards, and make eye contact with each student as he said their name; since students are creatures of habit who tend to sit in a similar area of class each day, I noticed he could also associate people with "regions" of the classroom and learned to look in the areas he associated with the name when trying to find a student. I suspect that this professor struggled a bit with facial recognition; however, he did an excellent job of compensating for this. I know he also sometimes took the cards home to look over, which is when I assume he used the facts about the person to also make them more memorable to himself. Students in turn appreciated his genuine effort to remember who they were and attendance and responses to questions he asked in class were both strong. He was considered a very engaging professor in a very difficult class and as a student I felt this tone started with his genuine effort to remember who we were; he then built on his own enthusiasm for the subject and carried us with him—we cared about the class because he cared about the topic and our learning the material. A pair of studies reported in 2000 found that the greatest predictor of college-student motivation in any class was the enthusiasm of the teacher (Patrick, Hisley and Kempler 2000). Studies have also shown that students learn more when they feel their teachers are engaged with the class and the material they are teaching (Allen, Witt and Wheeless 2006).

Another great strength this professor brought to the topic was his ability to find different ways to explain the same concept; while a handful of students always quickly followed everything he said, others of us struggled and seldom understood the first explanation of a new principle. He was very good at finding different ways of explaining, rather than just saying the exact same thing several times over. Those of us with language processing disorders particularly appreciated the way the professor worked to create examples that helped us form images in our mind of what he was talking about—when applicable he drew pictures on the chalk-board which facilitated this process.

I was in another class that was very challenging for me based on the use of numerical concepts—a formal logic class. This professor also excelled at finding a range of ways to explain the same idea. One of my favorite methods he used was to introduce an idea by turning it into a story about his Labrador retriever, who was apparently very given to working formal logic problems and participating in their outcome. Just as part of my brain was struggling with the numbers, another part was engaged by the relation of concepts to dogs—while this may seem odd, it made things much more bearable for myself and many other students who struggled with the information. The stories were just part of how he displayed his *enthusiasm* for the subject he was teaching and his engagement with students in the class.

Passion for a subject, in other words, and finding ways to share that passion with students, can engage a surprising range of students. Taking time to learn student names, telling stories that make the subject understandable in a different way, and finding a range of ways to communicate the same idea not only engage students because of their multi-modality, but because they help communicate how much a teacher cares about (1) what they are teaching; and (2) that the professor cares that students learn. I currently know a range of students who have taken classes with a professor who is notorious for getting slightly off-track in lecture with personal stories about the topic he is teaching. All these stories, however, relate back to the main topic and a number of students have told me they actually take notes on the stories themselves, because they find the stories help them remember the "point" that the professor was making. What I find particularly noteworthy is that some of the students who are most engaged by this professor are very intelligent and autistic—they respond to his astuteness and the detailed information he shares through his stories and the enthusiasm he has in relating these stories. To summarize, if one comes across as not being particularly excited or interested with the topic they are teaching, students will feed off of this lack of enthusiasm and mirror it in their own approach to the class.

My most vivid example of this came from an experience I had as a student, with a professor who had been teaching the same subject—a large introductory biology class—for a number of years. Even from my seat halfway back in the large lecture hall I could see that his notes were yellow with age. He was known to use the exact same notes to lecture from every time he taught the class, year after year. He basically read the notes, then carefully drew pictures on the board to illustrate a few key points with all the enthusiasm of someone who had spent a lifetime assembling cardboard boxes. The only passion he showed was on the rare occasions when he would have a grisly story to share about the topic of the day—his stories were of people becoming horribly infected by microscopic germs through everyday events like digging in their gardens without gloves or drinking contaminated milk.

There was a large failure/low grade rate in that class and I was not alone in primarily remembering the stories about the germs without recalling many of the "facts" I was supposed to be learning. While the class enhanced my obsessive compulsive fears, it did little for my understanding of biology, a topic I'd actually been interested in when I signed up for the course. One further disastrous biology class was all it took to convince me that I would not pursue a degree in marine biology. I switched to a major in geography, where I had found the professors uniformly interested in what they were teaching and willing to engage with students and their questions. In a day and age when there is increasing pressure to retain students in university and retain students-in-seats in each field of study, the capacity of the initial introductory courses to push students out of a field is still under-realized.

Teaching practices

Teachers and students working together in small classes can create the most diverse and memorable content. As I tell students, "I have just one point of view, you each bring specialized knowledge and experience to the topic that I do not have." It is none-the-less my responsibility as a teacher to create a learning environment and context where this range of views can be shared in a meaningful, non-threatening way while staying on-topic to the points of the day and the semester. What has been most helpful for me as a teacher is discussing with other teachers and successful mentors what does and does not work in creating this learning environment, sharing ideas of assignments that have and have not worked, and taking time to analyze what I have done that did and did not work in the classroom. I usually keep a teaching journal in which I write out what I will cover during the day, then after class I update this journal with what worked, what didn't, and what students responded to. I may teach the same class a number of times, but I am always "tweaking" what we do in the class and how we do it.

Pedagogical studies reinforce the importance of analyzing what we do in the classroom as teachers, as well as the value of reflecting on why we do things the way we do. In my experience as a student and a teacher, effective teachers do not cling to a practice based on the reasoning that "this is how we always do this," particularly when there are alternate ways to achieve a teaching goal. Sometimes we will not know without trial and error what methods will work best in achieving our teaching goals for a class. Other times, what works well with one group of students will not work with another. Classes have personalities, tones, and energy levels and these can vary from semester to semester—another reason why it can be so valuable to have the support of colleagues when we encounter a particularly challenging group of students. Building analytical self-reflection and collegial sharing of teaching practices and experiences into one's teaching routine are effective methods for maintaining a sense of balance. Being able to review how well an assignment worked with one group can sometimes be reassuring when a similar assignment flops with another group of students. At the same time, tracking responses to a type of assignment over the course of several semesters, one may discover they have come to rely on a way of doing something that is not working for the majority of students. This can be informative if one is willing to then adjust and attempt to find a more successful way of accomplishing the teaching goal with an adjusted assignment.

Perhaps one of the most important practices to implement, however, regardless of the size of a class one is teaching, is to allow students to see the enthusiasm one has for the topic they are teaching. As a student the teachers who stood out for me where the ones who left me with the impression that they found the topic they were teaching so fascinating or engaging that they knew I would share this opinion if I would allow myself to become engaged in the topic. I had memorable classes in areas where I had no particular aptitude—like economics and logic—because the professor's attitude made my engagement and subsequent learning possible. Professors who appeared to resent taking time to be in the classroom or interact with students on the other hand simply added to my burden as a disabled student who already struggled with a language processing disorder and anxiety. Two of the most discouraging attitudes a professor can display are apathy towards their subject and disdain for the students.

Administrative considerations

Not all topics will lend themselves to teaching styles that a humanities class might allow for. Professors who are engaged in a topic, though, can be found in every field. Administrators can encourage teaching which engages students by valuing teaching as much as they value research and publishing in the tenure process. What would happen if departments and schools within the institution formed committees that focus on best practices for teaching the core classes? What if departments began to sponsor lunches and seminars that were built around sharing best teaching practices; tips on how to achieve pedagogical goals; and lesson ideas that have proved effective? What if provosts and deans sponsored larger-scale events which allowed professors from different fields to share best practices and ideas, as well as opportunities to problem solve? What if each school within the college—Arts and Sciences, Technology, Education—sponsored their own on-campus lunch seminar where professors were facilitated in discussions of successful teaching practices/lessons, and new technology they were using on a yearly or semi-annual basis? What if administrators spent a conference discussing how they could each go home and put into practice policies and procedures that increased the value of successful teaching, the kind of teaching where students reported being engaged and learning?

An entire campus works together to create a tone where teaching is valued. At each level, professors, administrators and other staff can ask themselves, "What do I do which shows I value teaching?" It is also incumbent on the institution's administration to create an environment where teaching can flourish. Showing that teaching is valued requires more than words—it requires actions and, in many cases, these actions will need to include changes to policies. If teaching is not important as part of the faculty promotion process, it will remain undervalued. Why should professors work on continuing to improve their teaching? Why should departments care about their professors continuing to improve their teaching? With students facing increasing struggles, including an increasing presence of invisible disabilities amongst students wanting to be in college is not sufficient. Students with invisible disabilities require multi-modal presentation of information in order to be able to process new knowledge. Professors who are not encouraged to continue adapting to changes in students should not be expected to help retain these students.

The viability of an institution may increasingly come down to administrative support for effective teachers—a foundational aspect in retaining those with disabilities who will not remain in college if the status quo does not change. Legally, those colleges which do not provide the required support and adaptations required by disabled students will find themselves increasingly mired in litigation. As the disabled community becomes more educated about what they are legally able to expect from colleges, students' willingness to accept traditional exclusion is fading, replaced by costly court cases. Would an administration prefer to spend resources in preparing their institution to be universally prepared for diverse students, or to litigate when their lack of preparation leads to eventual legal battles? This is a question that each administration is facing and the plans that are made today will have long-term financial impacts based on how current administrators respond.

CHAPTER TEN
Institutional Policy

Administrators have traditionally had to deal with all the headaches that accompany running an institution of higher learning and in the past decade their jobs have only grown more complicated. Funding is stagnating while need for financial support grows. Retention and graduation rates, as well as concerns about time-to-graduation, are constantly under scrutiny. As families and governments struggle to pay for education there is increasing analysis of how many students an institution actually succeeds in guiding through the system and how long it takes on average for students to make the journey. Faculty request more support from staff due to challenging students and situations, while staff is called on to do more with fewer people and dwindling financial resources. Meanwhile a vocal social segment complains that academic institutions are out of touch with "the real world", and on one hand begrudges any funding colleges do get while on the other complaining that there are not enough skilled professionals to fill open jobs.

Neither faculty nor staff pursued careers in academics under the illusion that they would become wealthy. Those of us doing this work believe that education is important—critical in fact—to the future of our society. We believe that what we offer students through the process of studying and life at college will improve their future wellbeing and quality of life. We believe that what we do matters in a positive way to the students and communities whose lives we impact—which are basically all communities within our society. "An educated society is, fundamentally, a better society" being a fairly foundational idea most, if not all of us, share. We attempt to teach not just the subjects within the classroom, but how to live and work better within a diverse society and world; leadership skills; teamwork skills; how to give of oneself to others; and how to learn about oneself... among many other things. As individuals we volunteer both on campus and within our communities. We attempt to reach out to the world around us and share what we learn. The research done on our campuses drives developments in basically all fields from agriculture to greater understanding of the universe, biological nano-technology to better packaging of food. Now, in the face of increasing disability among the citizens we work with, including among ourselves as faculty and staff, we face complex and growing layers of additional concerns.

Some of the areas that administrators are constantly needing to re-evaluate are funding and staffing, which of course go hand in glove. Funding considerations in turn impact where and how money is spent on disability support, which in turn will increasingly impact retention of students, faculty, and staff. While there is longstanding concern about improving student retention, there appears to be far less concern regarding decreasing the rate of staff turnover. Failure to hold onto staff and as a result needing constant hiring initiatives and training for new staff are possibly the most under-recognized source of costs on college campuses (Bliss 2013; Peacock 2010). Yet many institutions do not adequately or accurately account for the cost of staff turnover.

Failure to provide the level of needed support for the mental health of students, faculty, and staff is another growing cost because it impacts retention rates and staff turnover. It is easier to demonstrate how lack of mental health support impacts student retention rates because there are actually studies conducted on this relationship, whereas again, staff retention and lack of mental health support are not focused on. The National Alliance on Mental Illness (NAMI) conducted a 2012 survey which found that 64 percent of students no longer in school said they had left for mental health related reasons; 50 percent of these students reported not having access to mental health services (Gruttadaro and Crudo 2012). Difficulties related to mental health contributed to student grades slipping, followed by loss of financial aid. Students also reported that when they could only be successful as part-time students, their financial aid was significantly impacted. It should also be noted that it is often difficult for students to afford mental healthcare and medication, even with *full* financial aid support, a level of aid for which part-time students are not eligible.

As NAMI's survey of students points out, "Since graduation rates are a key factor in ranking colleges in the closely followed *U.S. News* report on colleges, providing adequate college mental health services is a good investment of resources" (Gruttadaro and Crudo 2012, p.8). Yet, retention of "mentally ill" students is not a priority on the majority of college campuses. Chapter Seven showed that popular media emphasize incidents of violence committed by those with mental illness, creating the illusion that mentally ill people are violent people. Remember, the greatest predictor of violence is a familial relationship and/or substance abuse. It can be speculated that there is a direct relation, however, between the social impression that the presence of mentally ill students will lead to incidents like that at Virginia Tech, and the lack of effort made to retain mentally ill students. It seems plausible that many people believe they should be relieved that students with mental illness are not staying on campus, when the reality is that most of these students are dealing with mental illness related to anxiety and depression; they are not a danger to anyone, except perhaps themselves. Most, though, will just suffer and leave quietly without better access to mental health support. These are students who have the *potential* to be successful with appropriate support; however, the appropriate support is not currently in place on a significant number of campuses. This is a reality that administrators should be conscious of as they make funding decisions related to counseling services.

Mental health

For the past decade the World Health Organization (WHO) has been promoting the idea that mental health is an intricate part of a person's overall health and wellbeing (Herrman *et al.* 2005). This may sound obvious on the surface—mental health *is* part of our wellbeing. Consider though that in Western society at least, we have tended to split the mind and body into separate and separable entities. Socially, it is not uncommon for us to think that if someone looks physically healthy they should be capable of acting healthy and should carry on normal activities "without complaining." It is commonplace for those struggling with mental health issues to be told to "pull yourself together" or "get some exercise and you'll feel better." WHO is calling us to recognize that if a person is struggling with mental illness, all other aspects of their life will suffer, including their ability to work, house and care for themselves. From the point of view of employers, employees with mental illness are like employees with any other physical illness—they will not be as productive if there is no tolerance for their "recovery" or support for their treatment and maintenance of healthy habits.

Jacobson and Curtis began suggesting in 2000 that if we speak of *recovery* in treating mental health, then we are more likely to consider mental health like other physical illnesses; recovery in this case refers to the life-time path of treatment and working to remain productive that so many people with mental illness experience (Jacobson and Curtis 2000). To select some of their primary points outlining this concept of recovery:

- Recovery is a *process*.

- The course of that path is understood to be highly *singular* or *unique*.

- In contrast to the passivity of being a patient or a voiceless recipient of services, recovery is *active* and requires that an individual have personal responsibility for his or her own recovery, often in collaboration with friends, family, supporters, and professionals.

- A recovery orientation includes an emphasis on *choice*, a concept that encompasses support for autonomous action.

- The emotional essence of recovery is *hope*.

- A key theme is that of *meaning*, or the discovery of purpose and direction in one's life.

(Jacobson and Curtis 2000, p.335, emphasis original)

Part of recovery in treating mental illness for most people is maintaining their work identity. As was shown in Chapter Seven, those with mental illness are often creative, intelligent people who wish to continue their careers. Working can assist people in maintaining their sense of personal wellbeing as well as a sense of worth to their society. It also allows people to maintain financial independence. Jacobson and Curtis suggest that "service providers and administrators" may require ongoing education to understand their role in working with those in recovery as part of living with mental illness (Jacobson and Curtis 2000, p.336). What administrators need to consider, and where policy needs to be adapted is affected by how each administration is able to address the following considerations:

- Are policies implemented which *encourage education* regarding mental health for students, faculty, and staff?

- How many *opportunities* and how accommodating are the opportunities to become better educated about mental health on campus?

- Is *support* provided so that those outside professional counseling staff may become educated about mental health?

- Are *services* provided that support the mental health of faculty and staff in addition to supporting students?

- Which members of your administrative team have *experience* dealing with mental health issues personally? What have they learned from that experience that they have used to educate their campuses?

The World Health Organization's report on mental health points out that just as heart health improved by recognizing and changing influencing factors like smoking and diet, mental health can be better supported by recognizing influencing factors like access to work, education, housing, and child care. WHO's report states that mental health is "a state of wellbeing in which the individual realizes his or her own abilities, can cope with the normal stresses of life, can work productively and fruitfully, and is able to make a contribution to his or her community" (Herrman *et al.* 2005, p.2). WHO's concept of mental health is similar to the concept of being in recovery; we recognize that those who live with mental illness can supported in healthy social functioning by having adequate mental health support. WHO's underlying focus is the social mandate to assist this functioning by providing the treatment and support that allows the greatest number of people possible to be mentally healthy. While it may seem paradoxical, mental health does not equate to an absence of mental illness, but rather to adequate treatment and support, including medicine and/ or counseling, for those who require assistance in maintaining their mental health. As the earlier presented statistics have shown, mental illnesses including clinical depression and anxiety disorder are going to touch an increasing number of lives and families.

The framework WHO is suggesting takes into account that, "Mental health and mental illness are determined by multiple and interacting social, psychological and biological factors, just as health and illness in general" (Herrman *et al.* 2005, p.xviii). *Mental illness* is to some extent contextual. In other words, we may not agree on what makes someone mentally ill but we can come closer to agreeing on the elements of *mental health*. A person who hears the voice of God will be perceived differently by different cultural groups—that person might be called mentally ill, they might be called a prophet, or they might be called the head of one's religious movement. If that person can make rational decisions about their own welfare without harming others, then WHO would suggest that they are living with a level of mental health. As stated in WHO's report, "mental health implies fitness rather than freedom from illness" (Herrman *et al.* 2005, p.6). What WHO is proposing is not to focus on the truth content of a person's beliefs, but instead to recognize where a person requires support for their mental health.

Access to education and work are part of ensuring someone's wellbeing and thus supporting their mental health. *Legally*, governments around the world are clarifying that like all disabled people, those with mental illness are protected from discrimination. One of the implications of this legality for administrators is that even if the idea of having a mentally ill student in class or a work environment makes an employee uncomfortable, that person cannot be discriminated against. This is true regardless of the country one lives in. The same is true for maintaining non-discriminatory hiring and work environments. While hiring committees will seldom if ever know when a candidate also happens to live with mental illness, should a person's mental illness become known in the work environment, it is administration's duty to facilitate a non-hostile work environment. The reality is, everyone has met someone who is affected by mental illness—like all invisible disabilities mental illness is present in the workplace without our being aware of it. If an individual's mental health status becomes known in a classroom or work environment, it is the administration's responsibility to make sure the environment remains non-hostile, and non-discriminatory. Education for everyone involved might become part of the administration's responsibility.

WHO also predicts that by 2020, 15 percent of the world's population will be living with mental illness (Herrman *et al.* 2005, p.5). Governments, institutions, and communities will bear increasing costs if citizens/workers are not supported in maintaining their mental health—a fact which in and of itself will require many institutions to reevaluate their policies regarding the availability and use of mental healthcare. If one's college does not have access to adequate mental healthcare for students and employees, one can expect increasing attrition of students and employees. Education and work are important aspects of maintaining mental health; thus post-secondary institutions can expect that more students and staff living active lives, will also be living with mental illness. How often do policies and planning take these factors into account? It frequently appears that planning on campus related to mental health focuses primarily on preventing mass-killing, which practically speaking, though understandable, is not where the brunt of attention should be focused. Every campus already has students and faculty who would benefit from improved access to mental healthcare in order to support their mental health— better access to mental healthcare is also the policy which is most likely to *decrease* the odds that someone who needs care will remain untreated and become violent.

Reducing violence by implementing and enforcing conduct policies

A meta-analysis of studies that examined the relationship between mental illness and violence found that the same fact kept coming to the forefront—*those most likely to be violent are those with substance abuse issues*—regardless of if they had a mental illness or not (Fazel *et al.* 2009). This indicates that one of the more affective policy pieces for reducing violence on campus is to *increase access to diagnoses and treatment of substance abuse amongst both students and employees.* Whether it be drinking or drugs, the abuse of substances is the most accurate predictor of who has the capacity to become violent. Again, does the college's current policy and practices recognize this? Are practices in place to support treatment for substance abuse and possible underlying causes of this abuse? If, for example, a person is abusing substances in an attempt to self-medicate for depression or anxiety, how will the institution intervene in this cycle and what kind of support is available for the individual?

Policies which focus on behavior—what will be accepted and what will not—are both legally and practically speaking the policies which are most effective. However, administrators need to beware how these policies are framed, for example, punishing a student or employee for attempting suicide is not a good policy. The Judge David L. Bazelon Center for Mental Health Law in Washington D.C. advocates for colleges adopting policies which support mental health, rather than punishing those struggling with mental illness. As their web page states:

> Schools often respond to students with mental health needs in ways that violate the Americans with Disabilities Act (ADA).

Under the ADA, colleges and universities may not exclude students because of their mental health needs, except when the student cannot meet academic and behavioral standards even with treatment and other help (Bazelon Center 2012).

While the ADA is specific to the US, the underlying point is applicable to colleges outside the US, since governments globally have implemented laws which make it illegal to discriminate against those with disabilities. The Bazelon Center has drafted a policy which they make available online for all schools to copy and use. *Supporting Students: A Model Policy for Colleges and Universities* is available online through the Bazelon Center's website: www.bazelon.org. The Bazelon Center suggests that actively implementing a policy for working with and supporting mental health on campus is an important step that all colleges should be taking.

Students, faculty and staff need to be accountable under a standard of behavior that is clearly outlined in college-wide policy. In turn, these policies must be systematically enforced but fair. Policies that *address behavior before it becomes unacceptable* can contribute to retaining students and employees. Education first when possible should always be part of a school's mandate and this includes dealing with behavior related to the use of substances and conduct towards one another. Being very clear on when behavior is no longer acceptable is important to maintaining a safe campus. Being reasonable about when behavior is actually a danger to others, though, is also important. When someone's acts are aimed at himself, the university should be assisting with finding adequate mental health support, rather than trying to physically distance themselves from the person.

Employee workloads, retention, and support

As acknowledged in Chapters Eight and Nine, workloads are increasing for faculty and staff, even as salaries are frozen and funding for continuing education decreases. Now more than ever, administrators must consider where and how they will spend their money for assistive technologies, support staff, education, health services... everywhere really. Ironically, as has also been already pointed out, many administrations tend to underestimate the impact to their bottom line that staff turnover has. While some staff turnover is unavoidable and even desirable, high rates of turnover are costing money that many schools can ill afford. Part of what drives employees out of an institution is demoralization, which increases when budgets are tight and workloads heavy.

Writing for the *Harvard Business Review Blog*, Tony Schwartz observed that while over 100 studies have found that the most productive employees are those engaged with their work environment, only 20 percent of employees report being engaged with work; Schwartz points out that a company that does have engaged employees and is also successful is Google (Schwartz 2011). He suggests that this is not coincidence. Google has created an engaging work environment, employees are happy, they don't leave—and Google is successful. While some of Schwartz's suggestions for creating an engaging work environment might be expected—pay everyone a living wage for example—others might be a surprise:

- Provide healthy, high quality food at the lowest possible prices, including in vending machines.

- Clearly define what success in each specific job looks like—then allow as much autonomy as possible in achieving goals.

- Institute two-way performance reviews and allow those who are supervised to anonymously review their supervisors so that reprisals are not feared.

- Encourage supervisors to regularly recognize the positive contributions of their staff.

- Provide spaces and time for employees to rest and relax, which can increase their later-in-the-day productivity.

(Schwartz 2011)

In Western society we have come to believe that there is value in constant activity—or the appearance of always being busy. Yet, Schwartz is suggesting that employees who are encouraged to take breaks are more likely to be productive than employees working in an environment where the appearance of constant motion is valued.

How many college employees are currently working in environments where staff reductions or hiring freezes have resulted in fewer people doing more work? Saving money by reducing staff below critical levels is a policy that leads to the exact opposite of productivity and encourages employees to feel devalued. Not feeling appreciated in the work environment is one of the reasons employees look for new work environments—taking the institution's investment in training and institutional knowledge with them and leaving in their wake the cost for further hiring initiatives and training. Perhaps administrators need to readjust their cost–benefit analysis to consider whether money is more productively spent keeping and showing current employees they are valued (which incidentally increases morale) rather than spending such a large slice of their budget on hiring and training due to constant staff turnover. Unfortunately, the way budgets are allocated and reviewed may not favor this kind of cost–benefit analysis, meaning that there is a larger institutional challenge in accurately reflecting what institutionally is spent on staff turnover. Administrators need to ask themselves, what policies and practices do they need to implement in order to reflect accurately what staff turnover is costing the *institution*, rather than looking at departmental budgets in isolation. Decisions are also required about how far up the administrative ladder this information will rise, particularly as it impacts budget planning.

Expectations of faculty and requisite support

As with all other complex layers of what is happening on college campuses, the expectations of faculty have become broader and more complex. Socrates is often held up as a model of an ideal teacher, having taught his students by asking them questions that helped them discover answers. While there are some contexts where this "Socratic method" are useful, we have to consider that what is expected of teachers these days is not just getting students to think. Socrates was not required to grade papers, probably served on few committees, and did not appear to work in a "publish or perish" system of tenure. We still want professors to get students thinking. Asking thoughtful questions is not enough in and of itself to get that job done.

With the increasing diversity of students in the classroom—unlike when Socrates taught, education is no longer reserved for upper class male citizens—how a teacher makes knowledge available to students needs to be more complex, just as what students are responsible for knowing in a modern workplace has become more complex. We expect people to be able to communicate with people from a range of cultural and socioeconomic backgrounds, using technology that covers a range of media. At the same time the students arriving on campus may have fewer social skills, more uncommon disabilities, and require unique supports. Faculty are increasingly challenged by how to support the students who are arriving in their classrooms while also spending more time responding to individual struggling students during office hours and in the class. More and more students require repetition and multi-modal presentation of information in order to learn what is being taught. This requires more prep time for faculty.

As demands for more complicated technological support in the classroom increase, faculty are also requiring more IT support, as well as more opportunities for IT education for themselves. How often do administrators revise policies and procedures to reflect the increasing burden on faculty as they attempt to respond to these increasing demands on their limited time and resources? In tenure review, does the amount of time needed for being an effective teacher get credited with the same weight as publications or presentations, or committee work? If colleges are to retain a larger percentage of a more disabled student population, it would seem logical that faculty are going to play a key role in adapting classes to new needs. Thus, faculty will require support from their institutions. Support includes valuing the work—the time and effort—necessary to be an effective teacher given these changing demands. A failure by the institution to value effective teaching is going to further alienate disabled students, who already face struggles with learning.

Another obstacle towards retaining disabled students is the increasing use of *adjunct instructors* to teach, given that *adjuncts seldom have as much support or access to ongoing education as do full-time faculty*. Adjuncts may not even have office space, never mind opportunities for input into administrative priorities. How does administration support the adjuncts who teach on campus? Are they provided coordinated orientation that informs them of the support services available on campus, including the location and services available through disability services, counseling services, and learning centers? Do they have access to IT education? Do they have access to mental health education—or services if they have their own need for mental health support? Are they both invited to and given compensation for attending significant educational initiatives? Are educational opportunities available at times when adjuncts can reasonably be expected to be in attendance, given that many adjuncts teach multiple classes and for more than one institution in order to support themselves and their families? Colleges increasingly make use of adjuncts to help control costs— is the administration in turn providing the requisite support so that adjuncts are positioned to help the institution retain students?

Family expectations

Those of us familiar with college education have seen an increasing level of involvement of families, particularly parents, in their students' education. We have used terms like *helicopter parents*, to refer to the always hovering; *black-hawk parents*, who swoop in without warning; *lawn-mower parents,* who are even closer and more involved than helicopter parents. These terms have evolved to reflect experiences with the majority of parents. As with all majorities, however, this majority does not include everyone.

Donald Williams, Director of Counseling Services at Michigan Technological University has coined a term for another type of parent that we sometimes see: *dump truck parents.* (Mr. Williams introduced this concept to me during our conversation in the fall of 2013. What follows is my interpretation of Mr. Williams' idea.) Unlike the very involved parents, dump truck parents bring their student to campus and leave the student and all the student's unresolved issues and problems on campus, driving away and expecting the college to "fix" whatever issues their student has. I personally think dump truck parents come in at least two varieties: (1) those who do not wish to know anything but final grades—or perhaps graduation dates; (2) those who expect the employees of the college to take charge of their student: administer necessary medication; oversee a balancing of homework and social life; smooth the student's life-path resulting in successfully guiding the student to a profitable career; make sure the student is hired for that important first job. The second variety of dump truck parent will call to complain bitterly if their student is failing and demand that someone "do something".

Helicopter parents have spent years working with their children and will have specific suggestions for interventions that might help their child at particular points during the semester, given the kind of challenge they believe their child is facing. Dump truck parents have no constructive ideas, just demands. If a dump truck parent's child struggles, it is the college's fault, always. Dump truck parents have been "failed" by earlier education which did not successfully teach their student all the life skills necessary to be happy and successful; it is now the family's expectation that the college pick up this slack. Dump truck parents are famous for saying, "I'm paying good money for this education, I expect…" A statement which can be followed by any and all sorts of expectations, regardless of whether such expectations are reasonable.

Shortly after Don Williams first shared the idea of dump truck parenting with me, another colleague returned from a frustrating encounter with such a parent. The parent had cornered her in their student's on-campus housing and proceeded to yell at this colleague because of the student's impending failure of their semester classes. "This is ALL your fault!" the parent had yelled at the employee in the middle of a busy dormitory. My colleague explained that she had made multiple attempts to contact the student—and had emailed the parent on numerous occasions—however, there had been no response to these attempts at out-reach. The parent's response? Neither they nor their student should be responsible for maintaining communication— that was the employee's "job". One of the most frustrating aspects of dealing with dump truck parents is that they are not confined to logic or reasonableness in their expectations or responses. As a result, sometimes college employees are going to be used as verbal whipping-boys by parents. While it is always challenging to deal with upset families, it is even more frustrating when families lash out due to their own familial failings. Dump truck parents add stress to the work environment and increase the need for employees to have safe places to vent their own frustrations. Employees left to deal with dump truck parents without clear support from their administration are only going to be more demoralized and thus less effective in their work.

Disabled faculty and staff

Invisible disabilities are present among all populations of people, including faculty and staff. Flexibility and the capacity for negotiation are going to be foundational strengths of the college administrators of the future. Sometimes the best and brightest in a specialized field of study also live with disabilities like Asperger's syndrome, AD/HD, bipolar disorder…it is a myth that any of the invisible disabilities discussed in this book precludes a person from having a successful career in academics. Personally, I find it ironic when a colleague insists that, "Someone with that disability will never make it in the real world." The reality is, no matter where one works, one works alongside people who have invisible disabilities. What is changing is the legal obligation for employers to accommodate disabled employees rather than being able to fire them the moment a disability presents a complication in the person's personal or work life. In theory most people do not want to discriminate against the disabled; in practice as soon as someone has a life complication that interferes with how they do their work, it seems to be a gut instinct to say, "If you can't do the work, we'll hire someone who can."

Employers are now expected to make reasonable accommodations for those with disabilities. Sometimes these accommodations are actually fairly small. Take for example the office space that was redesigned so that a large portion of it was devoid of natural light. The handful of employees who worked there all began having increased incidents of headaches. One of these employees had medical documentation of chronic migraines and asked for some kind of relief in the work environment. As the immediate supervisor became very flustered and insisted that it wasn't fair to move this one person to a "better" spot in the office, the Office of Institutional Equity (OIE) on campus became involved. After reviewing the situation, the OIE made sure that full-spectrum light bulbs were used to replace the florescent bulbs in the work environment. As a result, all the employees had an immediate decrease in their incidence of headaches, including the person with migraines. Everyone's work environment was improved with a very low cost solution. Sometimes it will take multiple points of view to see where a solution to an accommodation request lies. Currently, though, all college campuses tend to employ at least one person who specializes in disability services and accommodations. Often campuses will employ several such people—at least one who specializes in working with students and at least one who specializes in working with the institution's employees. When an accommodation seems complicated and one turns to these professionals to seek advice, the challenge may prove to have a simpler solution than is immediately apparent.

Other times, solutions will grow out of conversations and meetings. Chapters Eight and Nine pointed out that sometimes the best solutions to a teaching challenge will come from discussing the context with others who teach in the same field. Teachers can share successful assignment designs and administrators can share successful ways they have found to meet new accommodation needs. Does the administration foster these conversations? Has the campus ever designed and implemented a series of seminars on the disability supports that are available on campus and asked for input on how to improve these supports? How often do administrators put these threads of discussion together amongst themselves, i.e.—how do we retain invisibly disabled students and employees in the face of more diverse disabilities present in college? How can we apply the elements of universal design to not just our physical campus spaces, but to our hiring and promotion practices?

This latter question is complex. Universally designing (UD) a campus means that disability is present among leaders on-campus. UD also requires a campus to hold up disability as a valued part of diversity, as well as reflecting that disability is itself a diverse range of experiences. If someone were to visit a campus, though, what signs would they see that disability is a welcome aspect of diversity? Would it be evident in class offerings? In availability of restroom spaces, transportation, housing, and dining areas? In technical support for multi-modal classrooms? In physical access to buildings?

If one's home campus were to be visited by a stranger who was to study the physical layout of campus, the promotion and tenure guidelines, the curriculum vitae of those in administration and leadership roles, the continuing education offered to faculty and staff, and the way communication is handled—would the visitor see indications that invisible disabilities are welcome on campus? That this type of diversity is valued? That the institution's administration is actively working to make the campus a learning and living environment for a diverse range of people?

What administrators may not realize is that they are already receiving such visitors to campus, people who have these very questions in mind. Every year invisibly disabled potential students, staff, and faculty visit campus and consider if a particular campus is the right fit for them. Economically, the biggest impact may be felt most directly when families choose the school that will be the best fit for their invisibly disabled student—and do not choose one's institution because as a family they do not find the institution's environment conducive to their invisibly disabled student's needs. One's institution is also limited from attracting bright and creative hires, when those with invisible disabilities do not see the potential for the kind of support they will need. Flexible schedules, health services, counseling, reasonable co-pays for medication, recognition and valuing of engaging teaching, valuing of individual strengths versus focus on personal weakness—these all impact not only which people will initially be attracted to an institution, but which employees will choose to stay.

Most foundationally, an administration sets the tone on campus. Of course everyone wishes to value excellence. How does the tone on one's home campus reflect the recognition that excellence includes the invisibly disabled, includes those with mental illness, learning disabilities, etc.? As administrators know, it is not just what one thinks or believes which matters—how one lives a value and is seen to enact that value has great impact. What are one's current actions doing to speak that invisible disability is welcome and supported on one's home campus? What areas can a campus identify and work on improving to make campus more supportive and welcoming of the invisibly disabled? Implementing policies and practices which make an environment more welcoming for the invisibly disabled will have the outcome of improving the environment for all citizens. A successful administration is one that finds ways to support and value the range of diversity on campus—it is important to recognize that the invisibly disabled are the largest growing diversity-group on campus. Remember, the number of invisibly disabled are growing. The institutions best prepared for this population are the institutions which will remain economically and academically most robust. Is your institution one of these?

References

ADDA: Attention Deficit Disorder Association (2012) "ADHD Fact Sheet." Available at www.add.org/?page=ADHD_Fact_Sheet, accessed on 7 December 2012.

ADAA: Anxiety and Depression Association of America (2012) "Understanding the facts of anxiety and depression is the first step." Available at www.adaa.org/understanding-anxiety, accessed on 12 December 2012.

Allen, M., Witt, P.L. and Wheeless, L.R. (2006) "The role of teacher immediacy as a motivational factor in student learning: using meta-analysis to test a causal model." *Communication Education 55*, 1, 21–31.

Alna, Y. and Susman, J.L. (2006) "Understanding comorbidity with depression and anxiety disorders." *Journal of American Osteopath Association Supplement 2*, 106, S9–S14.

Amen, D.G. and Carmichael, B.D. (1997) "High-resolution brain SPECT imaging in ADHD." *Annals of Clinical Psychiatry 9*, 2, 81–86.

American Psychiatric Asssociation (2013) *Diagnostic and Statistical Manual of Mental Disorders, Fifth Edition*. Washington, D.C.: APA.

Anderson, P.L. and Meier-Hedde, R. (2001) "Early case reports of dyslexia in the United States and Europe." *Journal of Learning Disabilities 34*, 1, 9–21.

Andre, F.E., Booy, R., Bock, H.L., Clemens, J., Datta, S.K. and John, T.J. (2008) "Vaccination greatly reduces disease, disability, death and inequity worldwide." *Bulletin of the World Health Organization 86*, 2, 140–146.

Andreasen, N.C. (1987) "Creativity and mental illness: prevalence rates in writers and their first-degree relatives." *American Journal of Psychiatry 144*, 10, 1288–1292.

Angst, F., Stassen, H.H., Clayton, P.J. and Angst, J. (2002) "Mortality of patients with mood disorders: follow-up over 34–38 years." *Journal of Affective Disorders 68*, 2, 167–181.

Baker, M. (2012) "What does it feel like to have bipolar disorder?" *Huffington Post*. Available at www.huffingtonpost.com/quora/what-does-it-feel-like-to_b_1391562.html, accessed on 19 March 2013.

Barnett, K.B. (2012) "After years on ADHD meds, searching for the authentic self." *Psych Central*. Available at http://blogs.psychcentral.com/my-meds/2012/06/after-years-on-adhd-meds-searching-for-the-authentic-self, accessed on 2 February 2013.

Baron-Cohen, S., Joliffe, T., Mortimore, C. and Robertson, M. (1997) "Another advanced test of theory of mind: evidence from very high functioning adults with autism or Asperger syndrome." *Journal of Child Psychology and Psychiatry 38*, 7, 813–822.

Baron-Cohen, S. and Klin, A. (2006) "What's so special about Asperger syndrome?" *Brain and Cognition 61*, 1, 1–4.

Bazelon Center (2012) "Campus mental health issues." Available at www.bazelon.org/Where-We-Stand/Community-Integration/Campus-Mental-Health.aspx, accessed on 18 April 2013.

"Berkhan, Oswald." ([1887] 2011) *Economy Point*. Available at www.economypoint.org/o/oswald-berkhan.html, accessed on 25 February 2013.

Biederman, J. (2005) "Attention-deficit/hyperactivity disorder: a selective overview." *Biological Psychiatry 57*, 11, 1215–1220.

Blake, R. (2006) "Employee retention: what employee turnover really costs your company." *WebProNews-Business. July (24)*, Available at www.webpronews.com/employee-retention-what-employee-turnover-really-costs-your-company-2006-07, accessed on 3 January 2013.

Bliss, W.G. (2013) "Cost of employee turnover." *The Advisor.* Available at www.isquare.com/turnover.cfm, accessed on 15 April 2013.

Brice-Heath, S. (2012) *Words at Work and Play: Three Decades in Family and Community Life.* Cambridge: Cambridge University Press.

Brown, T.A., Campbell, L.A., Lehman, C.L., Grisham, J.R. and Mancill, R.B. (2001a) "Current and lifetime comorbidity of the DSM-IV anxiety and mood disorders in a large clinical sample." *Journal of Abnormal Psychology 110*, 4, 585–559.

Buckley, P.F., Miller, B.J., Leher, D.S. and Castle, D.J. (2009) "Psychiatric comorbidities and schizophrenia." *Schizophrenia Bulletin 35*, 2, 383–402.

Bursztyn, A.M. (2007) *Praeger Handbook of Special Education.* Connecticut: Praeger Publishers.

Carey, B. (2012) "Father's age is linked to risk of autism and schizophrenia." *New York Times, August 22.* Available at www.nytimes.com/2012/08/23/health/fathers-age-is-linked-to-risk-of-autism-and-schizophrenia.html, accessed on 3 January 2013.

Center for Disease Control (2012a) "Autism spectrum disorders (ASDs)." Available at www.cdc.gov/ncbddd/autism/data.html 7, accessed on 7 December 2012.

Center for Disease Control (2012b) "Attention deficit hyper active disorder." Available at www.cdc.gov/nchs/fastats/adhd.html, accessed on 7 December 2012.

Center for Disease Control and Prevention (2013) "Symptoms and diagnoses: ADHD." Available at www.cdc.gov/ncbddd/adhd/diagnosis.html, accessed on 22 January 2013.

The Center for Universal Design, North Carolina State University (2008) "About the Center: Ronald Mace." Available at www.ncsu.edu/www/ncsu/design/sod5/cud/about_us/usronmace.htm, accessed on 16 March 2013.

Colorado State University (2011) "People and programs: Temple Grandin." Available at www.colostate.edu/templegrandin, accessed on 13 March 2013.

Coulter, A. (2013) "Guns don't kill people, mentally ill do." *Eagle Publications.* Available at www.humanevents.com/2013/01/16/ann-coulter-guns-dont-kill-people-the-mentally-ill-do, accessed on 22 March 2013.

Cooper, A. and Smith, E.L. (2011) "Homicide trends in the United States, 1980–2008: Annual rates for 2009 and 2010." *Bureau of Justice Statistics.* Available at http://bjs.gov/index.cfm?ty=pbdetail&iid=2221, accessed on 21 March 2013.

Courchesne, E. (1997) "Brainstem, cerebellar and limbic neuroanatomical abnormalities in autism." *Current Opinion in Neurobiology 7*, 2, 269–278.

Craddock, N., O'Donovan, M.C. and Owen, M.J. (2005) "The genetics of schizophrenia and bipolar disorder: dissecting psychosis." *Journal of Medical Genetics 42*, 3, 193–204.

Crichton, A. (1798) *An Inquiry into the nature and origin of mental derangement.* Available at http://adhdhistory.com, accessed on 22 January 2013.

Crockett, K. (2008) "Carol Greider, Scientist, Nobel Prize Winner." *The Yale Center for Diversity and Creativity.* Available at http://dyslexia.yale.edu/greider.html, accessed on 13 March 2013.

Darien, M. (2013) "Anxiety disorder goes beyond the blues." 7 May 2013. *Yahoo!News.* Available at http://news.yahoo.com, accessed on 10 May 2013.

De Bellis, M.D., Casey, B.J, Dahl, R.E., Birmaher, B., *et al.* (2000) "A pilot study of amygdala volumes in pediatric generalized anxiety disorder." *Biological Psychiatry 48*, 1, 51–57.

Dewey, J. (2012) *Democracy and Education.* Florida: Simon and Brown.

Disability Rights Education and Defense Fund (2007) "More laws." Available at http://dredf.org/laws/index.shtml, accessed on 13 December 2012.

DSM-IV Criteria for ADHD (2000) Centers for Disease Control and Prevention. Available at www.cdc.gov/ncbddd/adhd/diagnosis.html, accessed on 22 January 2013.

Dutton, J. (2007) "ADHD parenting advice from Michael Phelps' Mom." *ADDitude: Living well with attention Deficit. April/May2007.* Available at www.additudemag.com/adhd/article/1998.html, accessed on 6 February 2013.

Ebert, A. and Bar, K.J. (2010) "Emil Kraepelin: A pioneer of scientific understanding of psychiatry and psychopharmacology." *Indian Journal of Psychiatry 52*, 2, 191–192.

Edney, D.R. (2004) *Mass media and mental illness: A literature review.* Canadian Mental Health Association of Ontario. Available at www.ontario.cmha.ca/about_mental_health.asp?cID=7600, accessed on 19 March 2013.

Eisenberg, L. (2005) "Violence and the mentally ill: victims, not perpetrators." *Archives of General Psychiatry 62*, 8, 825–856.

English, B. (2012) "Autistic jazz savant graduates from Berklee." *The Boston Globe.* Available at www.boston.com/ae/music/articles/2012/05/12/autistic_jazz_savant_graduates_from_berklee, accessed on 11 February 2013.

Essau, C.A., Conradt, J. and Peterman, F. (2000) "Frequency, comorbidity, and psychosocial impairment of anxiety disorders in German adolescents." *Journal of Anxiety Disorders 14*, 3, 263–279.

Fazel, S., Galati, G., Linsell, L. and Geddes, J.R. (2009) "Schizophrenia and violence: systematic review and meta-analysis." *PLoS Med 6 (8) e1000120.* Available at www.ncbi.nlm.nih.gov/pmc/articles/PMC2718581/pdf/pmed.1000120.pdf, accessed on 10 April 2013.

Fearn, D. (2013) "ADHD and LD with no apologies or excuses." *Smart Kids with Learning Disabilities.* Available at www.smartkidswithld.org/parents-community/first-person/adhd-and-ld-with-no-apologies-or-excuses, accessed on 2 February 2013.

Fermier, S. and Lang, R. (2013) "Mentally ill shooter bought weapons legally." *WBAL News.* Available at www.wbal.com/article/97551/2/template-story/Mentally-Ill-Student-Shooter-Bought-Weapons-Legally, accessed on 22 March 2013.

Ferrer, E., Shaywitz, B.A., Holahan, J.M., Marchione, K. and Shaywitz, S.E. (2010) "Uncoupling of reading and IQ over time: empirical evidence for a definition of dyslexia." *Psychological Science 21*, 1, 93–101.

Firth, M. (2006) "Beckham reveals his battle with obsessive disorder." *The Independent, 3 April 2006.* Available at www.independent.co.uk/news/uk/this-britain/beckham-reveals-his-battle-with-obsessive-disorder-472573.html, accessed on 3 April 2013.

Fisher, L. (2012) "Anxious celebrities: stars with anxiety." *ABC News, 2 October 2012.* Available at http://abcnews.go.com/Entertainment/george-michael-tops-celebrities-anxiety/story?id=17366705#4, accessed on 3 April 2013.

Friends of Quinn (2012) "Exclusive video interview: Steven Spielberg on his dyslexia." Available at www.friendsofquinn.com/blog/post/exclusive-video-interview-steven-spielberg-on-his-dyslexia_9, accessed on 13 March 2013.

Frith, U. (1991) *Autism and Asperger Syndrome.* Cambridge: Cambridge University Press.

Ghaemia, S.N., Sachsb, G.S., Chiouc, A.M., Pandurangic, A.K. and Goodwina, F.K. (1999) "Is bipolar disorder still underdiagnosed? Are antidepressants overutilized?" *Journal of Affective Disorders 52*, 135–144.

Gillberg, C. and Billstedt, E. (2000) "Autism and Asperger syndrome: coexistence with other clinical disorders." *Acta Psychiatrica Scandinavica 102*, 321–330.

Gilman, L. (2005) "Career advice from powerful ADHD and LD executives." *ADDitude: Living well with attention Deficit. December/January.* Available at www.additudemag.com/adhd/article/754.html, accessed on 6 February 2013.

Grandin, T. (2013) "Dr. Temple Grandin's web page." Available at www.grandin.com accessed on 13 March 2013.

Greider, C. (2013) John Hopkins Medicine. "Carol Greider, PhD." Available at www.hopkinsmedicine.org/Research/awards/nobel/nobel_prize_greider.html, accessed on 13 March 2013.

Gruttadaro, G. and Crudo, D. (2012) "College Students Speak: A survey report on mental health." *National Alliance on Mental Illness (NAMI)* Available at www.nami.org/Content/ NavigationMenu/Find_Support/NAMI_on_Campus1/collegereport.pdf. accessed on 15 April 2013.

Hamilton, S.S. and Armando, J. (2008) "Oppositional defiant disorder." *American Family Physician* 78, 7, 861–866.

Herbert, M.R. (2010) "Contributions of the environment and environmentally vulnerable physiology to autism spectrum disorder." *Current Opinion in Neurology 23*, 2, 103–110.

Herrman, H., Saxena, S. and Moodie, R. (eds) (2005) *Promoting Mental Health: Concepts, Emerging Evidence, Practice.* Geneva: World Health Organization (WHO).

Hirschfeld, R.M. and Vornick, L.A. (2004) "Recognition and diagnosis of bipolar disorder." *Journal of Clinical Psychology 65*, 5–9.

"The History of ADHD Part 1: 1798" (2009) *The History of ADHD.* Available at http:// adhdhistory.com/the-history-of-adhd-part-1-1798, accessed on 22 January 2013.

Holmans, P., Green, E.K., Pahwa, J.S., Ferreira, M.A., *et al.* The Welcome Trust Case-Control Consortium (2009) "Gene ontology analysis of GWA study data sets provides insights into the biology of bipolar disorder." *American Journal of Human Genetics 85*, 1, 13–24.

Honkonen, T., Henriksson, M., Koivisto, A., Stengård, E. and Salokangas, R.K.R. (2004) "Violent victimization in schizophrenia." *Social Psychiatry and Psychiatric Epidemiology 39*, 8, 606–612.

Hunt, J. and Eisenberg, D. (2010) "Mental health problems and help-seeking behavior among college students." *Journal of Adolescent Health 46*, 1, 3–10.

Ingesson, S.G. (2007) "Growing up with dyslexia: interviews with teenagers and young adults." *School Psychology International 28*, 5, 574–591.

Jacobson, N. and Curtis, L. (2000) "Recovery as policy in mental health services: strategies emerging from the States." *Psychosocial Rehabilitation Journal 23*, 4, 333–341.

Jeste, D.V., Gladsjo, J.A., Lindamer, L.A. and Lacro, J.P. (2006) *Schizophrenia Bulletin 22*, 3, 413–430.

Kadesjo, B. and Gillberg, C. (2001) "The comorbidity of ADHD in the general population of Swedish school-age children." *Journal of Child Psychology and Psychiatry 42*, 4, 487–492.

Kaplan, A. (2012) "Anxiety disorders and ADHD: comorbidity the rule, not the exception." *Psychiatric Times.* Available at www.psychiatrictimes.com/conference-reports/apa2012/ content/article/10168/2069941, accessed on 2 April 2013.

Kaye, W.H., Bulik, C.M., Thornton, L., Barbarich, N. and Masters, K., Price Foundation Collaborative Group (2004) "Comorbidity of anxiety disorders with anorexia and bulimia nervosa." *American Journal of Psychiatry 161*, 12, 2215–2221.

Kendall, J., Hatton,D., Beckett, A. and Leo, M. (2004) "Children's accounts of attention deficit/ hyperactivity disorder." *Advances in Nursing Science 26*, 2, 114–130.

Kendlar, K.S., Neale, M.C., Kessler, R.C., Heath, A.C. and Eaves, L.J. (1992) "Major depression and generalized anxiety disorder same genes (partly) different environments?" *JAMA 49*, 9, 716–722.

King, W.M., Lombardino, L.J., Crandell, C.C. and Leonard, C.M. (2003) "Comorbid auditory processing disorder in developmental dyslexia." *Ear and Hearing 24*, 5, 448–456.

Kong, A., Frigge, M.L., Masson, G., Besenbacher, S., *et al.* (2012) "Rate of de novo mutations and the importance of father's age to disease risk." *Nature 488*, 7421, 471–475.

Kraepelin, E. (1920) *Manic Depressive Insanity and Paranoia.* Trans R.M. Barclay (1920) Scanned copy available at http://archive.org/stream/manicdepressivei00kraeuoft#page/n7/ mode/2up, accessed on 19 March 2013.

Lange, K.W., Reichl, S., Lange, K.M., Tucha, L. and Tucha, O. (2010) "Attention deficit, hyperactive disorder: The history of attention deficit hyperactivity disorder." *National Center for Biotechnology Information 2*, 4, available at www.ncbi.nlm.nih.gov/pmc/articles/ PMC3000907/#CR20, accessed on 22 January 2013.

Lucey, J.V., Costa, D.C., Adshead, G., Deahl, M., *et al.* (1997) "Brain blood flow in anxiety disorders. OCD, panic disorder with agoraphobia, and post-traumatic stress disorder on 99mTcHMPAO single photon emission tomography (SPET)" *British Journal of Psychiatry 171*, 4, 346–350.

Lyon, G.R., Shaywitz, S.E. and Shaywitz, B.A. (2003) "Defining dyslexia, comorbidity, teachers' knowledge of language and reading." *Annals of Dyslexia 53*, 1–14.

McClelland, G.M. and Teplin, L.A. (2001) "Alcohol intoxication and violent crime: implications for public health policy." *American Journal on Addictions 10*, (Suppl.), 70–85.

McIntyre, R.S., Konarski, J.Z, Soczynska, J.K., Wilkins, K., *et al.* (2006) "Medical comorbidity in bipolar disorder: implications for functional outcomes and health service utilization." *Psychiatric Services.* Available at http://ps.psychiatryonline.org/article. aspx?articleid=96924&link_type=googlescholar, accessed on 22 March 2013.

McKay, D.R. (2013) "6 reasons to make a career change." *About career planning.* Available at http://careerplanning.about.com/od/careerchoicechan/a/why_change.htm, accessed on 3 January 2013.

Mezies, L., Chamberlain, S.R., Laird, A.R., Thelen, S.M., Sahakian, B.J. and Bullmore, E.T. (2008) "Integrating evidence from neuroimaging and neuropsychological studies of obsessive-compulsive disorder: The orbitofronto-striatal model revisited." *Neuroscience and Behavioral Reviews 32*, 3, 525–549.

Mick, E., Biederman, J., Pandina, G. and Faraone, S.V. (2003) "A preliminary meta-analysis of the child behavior checklist in pediatric bipolar disorder." *Biological Psychiatry 53*, 11, 1021–1027.

Moffat, S. (2011) "Pokeman creator draws inspiration from autism." *Autism Key: Unlock the Mystery.* Available at www.autismkey.com/pokeman-creator-draws-creativity-from-autism, accessed on 21 January 2013.

Montgomery, S.A. (2009) *Handbook of Generalized Anxiety Disorder.* London: Springer Health Care.

Moore, D.R. (2006) "Auditory processing disorder (ADP): Definition, diagnosis, neural basis, and intervention." *Hearing, Balance and Communication 4*, 1, 4–11.

Mueser, K.T., Rosenber, S.D., Goodman, L.A. and Trumbetta, S.L. (2002) *Schizophrenia Research 53*, 1–2, 123–143.

Nalavany, B.A., Carawan, L.W. and Rennick, R.A. (2011) "Psychosocial experiences associated with confirmed and self-identified dyslexia: a participant-driven concept map of adult perspectives." *Journal of Learning Disabilities 44*, 1, 63–79.

National Center on Universal Design for Learning (2011) "About UDL." Available at www. udlcenter.org/aboutudl/whatisudl, accessed on 28 March 2013.

National Health Service (2012a) "Symptoms of obsessive compulsive disorder (OCD)" Available at www.nhs.uk/Conditions/Obsessive-compulsive-disorder/Pages/Symptoms. aspx, accessed on 14 March 2013.

National Health Service (2012b) "Schizophrenia." Available at www.nhs.uk/Conditions/ Schizophrenia/Pages/Introduction.aspx, accessed on 15 March 2013.

National Health Service (2013a) "Generalized anxiety disorder." Available at www.nhs.uk/ conditions/anxiety/pages/introduction.aspx, accessed on 14 March, 2013.

National Health Service (2013b) "Panic disorder." Available at www.nhs.uk/conditions/panic-disorder/pages/introduction.aspx, accessed on 14 March, 2013.

National Institute of Mental Health (2008) *Bipolar Disorder.* Maryland: U.S. Department of Health and Human Services.

National Institute of Mental Health (2009) *Schizophrenia.* Maryland: U.S. Department of Health and Human Services.

National Institute of Mental Health (2011) "Depression: What are the different forms of depression?" Available at www.nimh.nih.gov/health/publications/depression/what-are-the-different-forms-of-depression.shtml, accessed on 15 March 2013.

National Institute of Mental Health (2012a) "Anxiety disorders in children and adolescents: Fact Sheet." Available at www.nimh.nih.gov/health/publications/anxiety-disorders-in-children-and-adolescents/index.shtml, accessed on 12 December 2012.

National Institute of Mental Health (2012b) "Anxiety disorders: obsessive compulsive disorder." Available at www.nimh.nih.gov/health/publications/anxiety-disorders/obsessive-compulsive-disorder.shtml, accessed on 14 March 2013.

National Institute of Mental Health (2013a) "Anxiety disorders." Available atwww.nimh.nih.gov/health/publications/anxiety-disorders/introduction.shtml, accessed on 14 March, 2013.

National Institute of Mental Health (2013b) "The numbers count: mental disorders in America." Available at www.nimh.nih.gov/health/publications/the-numbers-count-mental-disorders-in-america/index.shtml, accessed on 19 March 2013.

O'Hare, T. and Sherrer, M. (2011) "Drinking motives as mediators between PTSD symptom severity and alcohol consumption in persons with severe mental illness." *Addictive Behaviors 36*, 5, 465–469.

Patrick, B.C., Hisley, J. and Kempler, T. (2000) "What's everybody so excited about?": The effects of teacher enthusiasm on student intrinsic motivation and vitality." *Journal of Experimental Education 68*, 3, 217–236.

Peacock, L. (2010) "Staff turnover costs UK £42bn a year." *The Telegraph*. Available at www.telegraph.co.uk/finance/jobs/8037869/Staff-turnover-costs-UK-42bn-a-year.html, accessed on 15 April 2013.

Pearson, J. (1996) "Suicide in the United States." *NAMI*. Available at www.nami.org/Content/ContentGroups/ENews/20023/March_20022/Suicide_in_the_United_States.htm, accessed on 22 March 2013.

Pittman, K.R. (1994) "Obsessive Compulsive Disorder in Western History." In E. Hollander, J. Zohar and D. Marazziti, B. Olivier (eds) *Current Insights in Obsessive Compulsive Disorder*, New York: John Wiley and Sons, pp.3–10.

Pittman, S.M. (2012) "Sinead O'Connor talks bipolar disorder and split with manager." *POLLSTAR*. Available at www.pollstar.com/news_article.aspx?ID=801367, accessed on 27 March 2013.

Politt, R., Pollock, J. and Waller, E. (2004) *Day to Day Dyslexia in the Classroom*. New York: Routledge.

Quily, P. (2008) "Howie Mandel has adult ADHD, does Adult ADHD is Real Awareness campaign." *Adult ADD Strengths*. (October 18, 2008). Available at http://adultaddstrengths.com/2008/10/18/howie-mandel-has-adult-adhd-does-adult-adhd-is-real-awareness-campaign, accessed on 6 February 2013.

Ramus, F. (2004) "Neurobiology of dyslexia: a reinterpretation of the data." *Trends in Neurosciences 27*, 12, 720–726.

Ramus, F., Pidgeon, E. and Frith, U. (2003) "The relationship between motor control and phonology in dyslexic children." *Journal of Child Psychology and Psychiatry 44*, 5, 712–722.

Ramus, F., Rosen,S., Dakiu, S.C., Day, B.L., Castellote, J.M., White, S. and Frith, U. (2003) "Theories of developmental dyslexia: insights from a multiple case study of dyslexic adults." *Brain: A Journal of Neurology 126*, 4, 841–865.

Recker, K. (2012) "The true cost of replacing an employee." Blog—*Executive Development. June 7*, Available at http://info.execdev.uni.edu/blog/bid/110182/The-True-Cost-of-Replacing-an-Employee, accessed on 3 January 2013.

Richlan, F., Kronbichler, M. and Wimmer, H. (2009) "Functional abnormalities in the dyslexic brain: a quantitative meta-analysis of neuroimaging studies." *Human Brain Mapping 30*, 10, 3299–3308.

Rihmer, Z. (2007) "Suicide risk in mood disorders." *Current Opinion in Psychiatry 20*, 1, 17–22.

The RL Mace Universal Design Institute (1998) "A brief history of universal design." Available http://udinstitute.org/history.php, accessed on 16 March 2013.

Rowa, K. and Antony, M.M. (2008) "Generalized Anxiety Disorder." In W.C. Craighead, D.J. Miklowitz and L.W. Craighead (eds) *Psychopathology: History, Diagnosis, and Empirical Foundations.* New York: John Wiley, pp.78–114.

Rowling, J.K. (2001) *Harry Potter and the Prisoner of Azkaban.* New York: Scholastic Press.

Rowling, J.K. (2007) "A Year in the Life." *YouTube.* Available at www.youtube.com/watch?v=p6-6zaa4NI4, accessed on 27 March 2013.

Rowney, J., Hermida, T. and Malone, D. (2010) "Anxiety disorders." *Cleveland Clinic Center for Continuing Education.* Available at www.clevelandclinicmeded.com/medicalpubs/diseasemanagement/psychiatry-psychology/anxiety-disorder, accessed on 14 March 2013.

Saks, E.R. (2013) "Successful and schizophrenic." *The New York Times.* Available at www.nytimes.com/2013/01/27/opinion/sunday/schizophrenic-not-stupid.html?_r=0, accessed on 27 March 2013.

Santosa, C.M., Strong, C.M, Nowakowska, C.N., Wang, P.W., Renicke, C.M. and Ketter, T.A. (2006) "Enhanced creativity in bipolar disorder patients: A controlled study." *Journal of Affective Disorders 100*, 2007, 31–39.

Sasson, Y., Chapa, M., Harari, E., Amitai, K. and Zohar, J. (2003) "Bipolar comorbidity: from diagnostic dilemmas to therapeutic challenge." *International Journal of Neuropsychopharmacology 6*, 2, 139–144.

Schwartz, T. (2011) "The twelve attributes of a truly great workplace." *Harvard Business Review Blog Network.* Available at http://blogs.hbr.org/schwartz/2011/09/the-twelve-attributes-of-a-tru.html, accessed on 15 April 2013.

Schwarz, A. (2013) "Drowned in a stream of prescriptions." *New York Times.* Available at www.nytimes.com/2013/02/03/us/concerns-about-adhd-practices-and-amphetamine-addiction.html?emc=eta1, accessed on 4 February 2013.

Shore, S. (2003) *Beyond the wall: Personal experiences with autism and Asperger syndrome.* Kansas: Autism Asperger Publishing Company.

Smoller, J.W. and Finn, C.T. (2003) "Family, twin, and adoption studies of bipolar disorder." *American Journal of Medical Genetics 123C*, 1, 48–58.

Srivastava, S., Childers, M.E., Baek, J.H., Strong, C.M., *et al.* (2010) Toward interaction of affective and cognitive contributors to creativity in bipolar disorders: A controlled study. *Journal of Affective Disorders 125*, 2010, 27–34.

Strine, T.W., Mokdad, A.H., Balluz, L.S., Berry, J.T. and Gonzalez, O. (2008) "Impact of depression and anxiety on quality of life, health behaviors, and asthma control among adults in the United States with asthma, 2006." *Journal of Asthma 45*, 2, 123–133.

Svartdal, F. and Iversen, T. (1989) "Consistency in synesthetic experience to vowels and consonants: Five case studies." *Scandinavian Journal of Psychology 30*, 3, 220–227.

Tartakovsky, M.C. (2009) "Media's damaging depiction of mental illness." *PsychCentral.* Available at http://psychcentral.com/lib/2009/medias-damaging-depictions-of-mental-illness/all/1, accessed on 19 March 2013.

TED Ideas worth spreading (2007) "Richard Branson." Available at http://blog.ted.com/2007/10/09/richard_branson, accessed on 13 March 2013.

Temple, E., Deutsch, G.K., Poldrack, R.A., Miller, S.L., *et al.* (2003) "Neural deficits in children with dyslexia ameliorated by behavioral remediation: Evidence from functional MRI." *Proceedings of the National Academy of Sciences of the United States of America 100*, 5, 2860–2865.

Teplin, L.A., McClelland, G.M., Abram, K.M. and Weiner, D.A. (2005) "Crime victimization in adults with severe mental illness: Comparison with the National Crime Victimization Survey." *Archives of General Psychiatry 62*, 8, 911–921.

TIME Asia (2013) "Interview with Satoshi Taijiri." pokédream . Available at http://pokedream.com/pokemon/infocenter/tajiri.php, accessed on 13 March 2013.

Tonnessen, F.E. (1997) "How can we best define 'dyslexia'?" *Dyslexia 3*, 78–92.

Tull, M. (2009) "Ways of coping with anxiety." Posted on About.com.Health. 14 May 2009. Available at http://ptsd.about.com/od/selfhelp/tp/anxietycoping.htm, accessed on 10 May 2013.

United Nations. "Convention and optional protocol signatures and ratifications." Available at www.un.org/disabilities/countries.asp?navid=17&pid=166, accessed on 13 December 2012.

Voeller, K.S. (2004) "Attention-deficit hyperactivity disorder (ADHD)" *Journal of Child Neurology 19*, 10, 798–814.

Wagner, R.F. (1973) "Rudolph Berlin: originator of the term dyslexia." *Bulletin of the Orton Society 23*, 1, 57–63.

Warnke, A., Schutte-Korne, G. and Ise, E. (2012) "Developmental Dyslexia." In M.E. Garralda and J.P. Raynaud (eds) *Brain, Mind, and Developmental Psychopathology in Childhood.* Maryland: Jason Aronson Inc., pp.173–198.

Willey, L.H. (1999) *Pretending to be Normal.* London: Jessica Kingsley Publishers.

Wing, L. (1998) "The History of Asperger's Syndrome." In E. Schopler, G.B. Mesibow and L.J. Kurice (eds) *Asperger Syndrome or High-Functioning Autism?* New York: Plenum Press, pp.11–28.

World Health Organization (2008) "Vacination greatly reduces disease, disability, death and inequality worldwide." Available at www.scielosp.org/scielo.php?pid=S0042-96862008000200016&script=sci_arttext&tlng=pt., accessed on 13 December 2012.

Yu-Feng, Z., Yang, H., Chao-Zhe, Z., *et al.* (2007) "Altered baseline brain activity in children with ADHD revealed by resting-state functional MRI." *Brain and Development 29*, 2, 83–91.

Zulyen-Wood, S.V. (2011) "Life after war: perspectives on PTSD from Rhode Island veterans." *Campus Progress Journalism Network.* Available at http://campusprogress.org/articles/life_after_war_perspectives_on_ptsd_from_rhode_island_veterans, accessed on 14 March 2013.

Index